❧ CREATING
❧ CUSTOMER
❧ DELIGHT

ॐ CREATING
ॐ CUSTOMER
ॐ DELIGHT

THE HOW AND WHY OF CRM

Rakesh Seth ■ Kirti Seth

Response Books
A division of Sage Publications
New Delhi/Thousand Oaks/London

First published in 2005 by

Response Books
A division of Sage Publications India Pvt Ltd
B-42, Panchsheel Enclave
New Delhi 110 017

Sage Publications Inc	**Sage Publications Ltd**
2455 Teller Road	1 Oliver's Yard
Thousand Oaks	55 City Road
California 91320	London EC1Y 1SP

Published by Tejeshwar Singh for Response Books, typeset in 11/13 pt Baskerville BE Regular by Innovative Processors, New Delhi, and printed at Chaman Enterprises, New Delhi.

Library of Congress Cataloging-in-Publication Data

Seth, Rakesh, 1958–
  Creating customer delight: the how and why of CRM/Rakesh
  Seth, Kirti Seth.
        p. cm.
  Includes index.
  1. Customer relations—Management. I. Seth, Kirti, 1966– II.
  Title.
  HF5415.5.S48 2005   658.8′12—dc22   2005002411

ISBN: 0–7619–3296–8 (PB)   81–7829–507–5 (India–PB)

Production Team: Leela Kirloskar, R.A.M. Brown,
                    Neeru Handa and Santosh Rawat

To
all our customers—
family, friends, clients
and
colleagues

Contents

Foreword

I have always been skeptical about Customer Relationship Management (CRM). Not because it's a fad but because organizations haven't really paid enough attention to implementation. Rakesh and Kirti Seth's book, *Creating Customer Delight: The How and Why of CRM*, puts such doubts to rest because it's a cogent handbook on managing customer satisfaction by implementing it efficiently. Peppered with case studies and 40 years of field experience, the authors have come up with a strategist's trump card.

Why is it important to know the customer better? The Seths provide the trigger points and dwell on them in detail throughout the book. The trigger points: greater competition and wider consumer choice; fragmentation of the media and the advent of new media; rise of the 'me' generation; technological advances, especially the cell phone and the web; existing customers as future customers; and internal-customer satisfaction.

What impressed me was the objective of the study, adequately spelt out in the authors' preface, 'CRM provides the buffer between business and business cycles. And since these will happen, it is important to practice CRM.'

But I do want to leave readers with an interesting thought. You cannot create a CRM culture until you empower the last mile. And that is where the customer interfaces with the organization the most. The last mile is the toughest mile in the CRM marathon. And organizations which make it the easiest stretch by empowering employees, are sure to win.

One of the biggest experiences that I have had in CRM is in my present stint in Indiatimes.com, India's largest portal. Here, CRM is real time since you can map customer preferences online. The success of such an online CRM system hinges on the level of intelligence you can build into that system. How do you intelligently predict what the customer will buy when he transacts with you a second time round? How do you manage his just-in-time urgency with your backend logistics? And how do you create and ignite his latent demand with fresh offerings?

CRM gave us all these answers at Indiatimes. You will not imagine the impact of our customer satisfaction management unless you fathom the benefits of synergy from two hot customer linkages: Internet+CRM. True, we have improved our revenues and margins substantially. But the biggest benefit from CRM is our ability to recognize our customer instantly and increase his/her interactions with us with constantly improving technology. Little wonder then that I insist that every senior management prospect must also be interviewed through the prism of CRM. For, the knowledge of CRM defines our entire value chain.

I am sure that the Seths have already thought of a sequel to delight readers with their enormous field experience.

Mahendra Swarup
CEO—Times Internet

Preface

WITH today's customer spoilt for choice, customer delight and not just customer satisfaction is what is needed for business success and prosperity. Unfortunately, many enterprises and managers have still not realized this a decade after liberalization in India. Some of those that have, may not have the tools to achieve customer delight scientifically, systematically and regularly. Students of CRM may also want a reference book based on the Indian context. It is to this audience that *Creating Customer Delight: The How and Why of CRM* is addressed.

We wrote this book to share our varied experiences in CRM in the hope that there will be greater effort in achieving customer delight and that others could benefit from our experience. In fact, when the 1–600 service was started by Mahanagar Telephone Nigam Limited (MTNL) in November 1998, we co-founded a CRM company—Finedge India (P) Ltd—with a mission 'to help our clients achieve outstanding customer interactions effectively and efficiently'. The goal was to provide customers with a toll-free number, where they could call in for information or complaints, similar to what is available in the West. It is a sobering thought when one looks around and sees how much money companies spend in talking to the customer (through media) and how little they devote to allowing the customer to communicate with them. This is in spite of the fact that the consumers' responsiveness to the company would be so much greater when he wants to communicate with it. A brilliant opportunity to try and capture a customer for life and yet, so many companies regard it as a problem! For instance, when we were trying to convince the heads of marketing of two of the best known (and respected) brands to take on a helpline, they said they did not want to because they did not want consumers to complain!

Clearly, the need for CRM and the need for consistency and excellence at all customer touch points needs to be explained.

Customer delight is possible only by knowing the customer in detail and interacting with him/her—something the chapters on database management, call centres and technology address.

Managers must seek to manage to maximize customer delight for all its customers. And they must do it in a manner that leaves some goodwill reserves for each cluster of customers, should there be any temporary dissatisfaction. CRM will be truly successful when so much delight has been created, that even if there is some dissatisfaction, the goodwill is enough to ensure continued customer engagement till delight is provided again. Thus, CRM is like the buffer between business cycles.

We have tried to keep the book simple with as many real-life examples as possible.

We hope you find it interesting and useful, and enjoy reading it as much as we did writing it.

We would welcome your comments on the book or sharing your CRM views and experiences with us. That would truly delight us!

You can contact us at rseth@finedgeindia.com

Rakesh Seth
Kirti Seth

Acknowledgements

W E would first like to acknowledge that we are each other's best customers. Our shared work experience of 40 years has contributed to the writing of this book, and we'd like to thank each other for this mutual effort.

We also thank three of our colleagues from Finedge India (P) Ltd—Paresh Tripathy for the section on technology, Vishal Mehan for inputs on call-centre quality and K. Kumar for helping with the logistics.

Finally, we'd like to thank Leela Kirloskar of Response Books, Sage Publications India Pvt Ltd—our primary customers for the book for engaging with us, and our readers for giving us their custom.

Introduction

THE road to CRM is not a new one. Your neighbour-hood grocer has practiced it for years. Sukhia, the *dhabawala* at St Stephens, practiced it when he allowed credit on a select basis to his customers and chatted with each one of them so that his place became a popular hang-out. *The important thing to note here is that credit was given on a select basis.*

However, CRM was not followed in India by the bureaucracy or even by industry, thanks to the constraints of the licence *raj*. In this millennium, the challenge is to change this mindset where it exists, which it still does in some of the most progressive companies in India.

Even at the height of the 'supplier's market' there were instances of aggressive CRM.

In the 1930s, for example, Nestle Milky Bar had a collection of pictures relating to the King of England and the Emperor of India . The wrapper of each bar of choco-late had to be collected and pasted in an album specially printed for the purpose.

For years, it was known that infant milk formulae were misused as whiteners since there was no dairy creamer or whitener in the market. By understanding the consumer habit, Nestle developed a new product simply by removing the vitamins and minerals from the infant milk formula, putting it in a pack which clearly showed whitening use and called the product 'Everyday Dairy Whitener'. At that point of time, such a product did not exist anywhere in the world and the term 'dairy whitener' was coined by Nestle's marketing group. The product, which was launched barely six months after the project was conceived (in July 1986), was a sell out from the very first day. No market research was conducted prior to the launch except product tasting in the test kitchen! The entire project was based on Nestle's knowledge of the consumer. 'Everyday Dairy Whitener' became Nestle's highest turnover product in just four years and forced competition to launch 'me-too' whiteners. By understanding your customer well, it is possible to adapt your organization to meet his/her needs. Customer knowledge will ensure you need know or do little else!

Another example of using consumer knowledge to telling effect is Tesco, UK's largest retailer. In 1995, Tesco introduced a loyalty card, which gave consumers 1–2 per cent value points on their purchases, which could be redeemed later at Tesco stores. The loyalty cards used were smart cards, which stored all the purchase data. This was analysed by Tesco which then offered tailor-made products. Imagine a situation where you are a brand marketer where the retailer who also has a private label knows how much Nescafe (and which Stock Keeping Unit [SKU]) Mrs Smith consumes every month and you don't! Imagine the possibilities for Tesco's category manager— he is better informed and in the information age, knowledge is power! This initiative helped consolidate

Tesco's position as the UK's No. 1 retailer and forced competition to launch similar cards. Tesco has not looked back since.

But CRM is not only about customer insights, understanding and offers. It involves providing service and information about the product to a customer when she needs it—like the 1–800 service abroad. It encompasses all aspects of the brand offerings including the 8 Ps, which are discussed later in the book.

CRM seeks to provide customer delight. It is the road from brand trial to brand usage to brand advocacy. It is a passion to please the customer and a search for excellence and quality in every interaction with her. CRM is about human interactions (aided by technology) and behaviour.

Successful CRM is what successful enterprise is all about. Every other discipline is secondary, be it marketing, finance, sales or IT. Managing external and internal customers individually and together is what is required. For example, sales must balance its external customer's needs with the internal needs of production and finance. Marketing must balance advertising product claims with product delivery and product development, and execute its strategies based on its internal customers—sales, finance and production.

The interesting thing to keep in mind is that the customer keeps changing at an increasingly faster pace and the change is influenced in part by how you and other competitors and touch points serve them. So, the challenge is to keep serving an ever-changing set of customers because even the needs, wants and requirements of the existing ones keep changing. For an enterprise to exist it must have/retain customers. Practising CRM in order to exceed customer expectations is the answer to ensuring customer delight.

For an organization to effectively practice CRM, it is critical to be informed and updated, as the tools for CRM, IT in particular, are also changing and evolving. To use Keynesian terminology, 'demand is influencing supply and supply is influencing demand and since both are influencing each other it is a never ending process'.

The road to customer delight is one in which the journey itself is a pleasure because it is a road which is ever-evolving and growing. Let us travel it!

Chapter 1

The Growing Need for CRM

MARKETING practice and philosophy has evolved over time. Initially, the focus was on building 'the better mouse-trap'. That was the age of invention and innovation, when companies produced truly innovative products like the telephone, the telefax, instant coffee, the refrigerator and so many other products we take for granted today. They brought these products to the market and grew and developed the market for them. The challenge was to develop the new product and communicate its availability and benefits to the target audience.

Then 'me-too' products were introduced and the markets became more competitive. Success became dependent upon not only how your product performed but how it performed vis-à-vis competition. The market rapidly became crowded and one had to stand out against competition.

This was the era when 7 Up as the 'uncola' drink became an outstanding success. It positioned itself as unique compared to the large majority of drinks viz. colas. Similarly, the Avis campaign, 'We are No. 2. Why rent with us. Because we try harder', backed with a vigorous service drive, propelled that company to almost No. 1. Till the market leader Hertz repartee: 'Hertz because winners do not come second'! Both these were cases of competitor-centric marketing.

Nothing personifies competition-centric marketing better than the cola wars, when Pepsi and Coke marketing responses are determined by each other—remember when Coke became the official drink of the cricket world cup, Pepsi launched the hugely successful 'Nothing official about it' campaign? Linked to the competitive situation (and, of course, to daily Indian life as well)! Another example is the Surf counter-attack to Nirma, with Lalita*ji* focusing on value for money and quality vs a simply low price.

When you're only No.2, you try harder. Or else.

Little fish have to keep moving all of the time. The big ones never stop picking on them.

Avis knows all about the problems of little fish.

We're only No.2 in rent a cars. We'd be swallowed up if we didn't try harder.

Avis can't afford to relax.

There's no rest for us.

We're always emptying ashtrays. Making sure gas tanks are full before we rent our cars. Seeing that the batteries are full of life. Checking our windshield wipers.

And the cars we rent out can't be anything less than spanking new Plymouths.

And since we're not the big fish, you won't feel like a sardine when you come to our counter.

We're not jammed with customers.

However, Pepsi has realized to its cost that the focus now needs to be on the consumer and not so much the competition. Pepsi was happy that it was the largest selling cola in India and continued to focus on taking the share from Coke, rather than on focusing on growing the market; which role Coke with its traditional market leader mindset did with the launch of the 200 ml bottle at Rs 5 and its massive campaign that the dealer does not overcharge. With this campaign, Coke, in 2003, for the first time, grew faster than Pepsi.

Another example of the market leader trying to grow by doing its best to expand the market is a Maruti 2004 campaign, where it directly exhorts two-wheeler users to upgrade to a Maruti by focusing on the Rs 2,200 only Equal Monthly Instalments (EMIs) at which it is available. 'Do not get wet', the Maruti owner tells a scooterist passing by in the TV ad!

In much of the developed world and especially in a developing country like India, where consumers need to be educated into new consumption habits and the challenge is to increase per capita consumption rather than take the share directly from competition, the focus needs to be on developing the market. Indeed, both cola companies now define 'share of throat' as their business and have got into the water and fruit juice business, while Coke has even introduced their Georgia brand of hot coffee and tea.

In order to appreciate the potential offered by the great Indian middle class, one needs only to look at some comparative statistics with other countries (Table 1):

Hertz has a competitor who says he's only No. 2.

That's hard to argue with.

Hertz	No. 2
1. A car where you need it.	**1. We try harder.**
We're in big towns like yours. In little towns like Whitefish, Montana. We're at every major airport in the United States and at most of the smaller ones. In fact, if an airport is served by a commercial airline, 97 chances out of 100 it'll also be served by Hertz. Or by a Hertz office within 20 minutes of it. In all, we have over 2,900 places throughout the world where you can pick up or leave a car. Nearly twice as many as No. 2.	
2. What kind of car would you like?	**2. We try harder.**
When you rent from Hertz, you're less likely to get stuck with a beige sedan when you want a red convertible. We have over twice as many cars as No. 2.	

We have Fords, Mustangs, Thunderbirds, Lincolns and everything else in between.	
3. Who's perfect?	**3. We try harder.**
When you rent a car from us and our service is not up to Hertz standards—if we goof—we give you $50 in free rentals. Plus an apology. No. 2 gives you a quarter. Plus an apology.	
4. Hot line.	**4. We try harder.**
When you're in one city and you're flying to another city and you want to have a car waiting when you arrive and you want it confirmed before you leave, we can do it. Instantly. In 1,038 cities. No other rent-a-car company can do this. The major reason we can do it is because we recently installed one of the world's most advanced reservations systems.	
5. No. 2 says he tries harder. Than who?	**5.**

competitor who was riding off with your customers and your dignity. Hertz finally did it. Their new campaign came out swinging and transformed a one-sided argument into an old-fashioned street brawl. Jim Durfee's caustic copy demolished the Avis platform. After the appearance of these ads, the Avis campaign never again attained the same level of intensity and success that it had enjoyed previously.

Table 1: Country Comparison

Per '000	India	US	Japan	Russia	China	Brazil	Singapore
TV Sets	83	835	731	538	312	349	300
Radios	120	2,117	956	418	339	433	672
Landlines	38	667	597	243	137	218	471
Cellular	6	451	588	38	110	167	724
PCs	6	625	349	50	19	63	508

Note: Figures per '000 pop; all relate to 2001.

Source: *A Statistical Outline of India, 2003–04* by Tata Consultancy Services (TCS) Ltd.

While there is direct competition for market share in India, the real challenge is to obtain a greater share of the customers' wallet, with banks and other financial institutions vigorously competing with each other to provide consumer finance and Indians increasingly developing the 'consume now pay later' mentality of the West. Strange as it may seem, the competition for a car is also from a house because both are available at EMIs and while that of a car is for 3–6 years, that of a house or flat is up to 25 years!

Similarly, a premium soap like Lux Supreme faces competition not only from other premium soaps but from consumer non-durables and holidays too because by downgrading, for instance, the consumer can generate a surplus for either a holiday or a small kitchen appliance. Only a few years ago, the consumer finance market was not so well developed and you had to forego consumption first and save, and then only could you buy durables or spend money on holidays.

Many years ago, in his article 'Marketing Myopia', Theodore Levitt emphasized the need for focusing on the consumer. He highlighted that in the US, the railways forgot they were not in the railroad business but in the transportation business (consumer needs) and they needed to consider the airlines and roadways as competition too, and not regard themselves as a monopoly. Forget the consumer at your peril!

It is important to realize what your true competition is. This definition must be in terms of customer needs and wants. For example, the competition to Delhi's Mahanagar Telephone Nigam Ltd (MTNL) is not only from Bharti (landlines) but from Airtel, Hutch, Idea and Reliance cellular companies.

Again, the Bombay Electric Supply Co. (BSES), or Reliance Energy as it is now called, is not really a complete monopoly. It faces competition directly from diesel gensets and solar energy devices. It is in the 'energy' business. So, it faces indirect competition from whatever the alternative uses to electric energy are—including no usage. For example, if children decide to play games on a cell phone rather than watch a TV programme, it not only impacts the TV industry, it impacts the electricity industry too!

It is important to figure out where on Maslow's need hierarchy your products figure—need, comfort or luxury. And the interesting point is that an air conditioner (AC) may be a need for someone, a comfort for another and a luxury for a third! How many consumers are there in each segment for the industry and your brand? This is the understanding upon which your strategies must be based.

Given the competition, it should be obvious that companies need to be customer focused.

Even MTNL, which till not so long ago required 'contacts' or a 'nothing official about it' effort to get a telephone connection, is now offering to waive connection charges and offering to give lines promptly and even appointing relationship managers for its large customers.

Indeed, there is a growing realization that a consumer, in the words of Mahatma Gandhi is 'not an interruption of our work but the purpose of it'. There is a realization that a business's most valuable asset is its customers and there is a debate on how the brand equity or franchise of a company is to be valued in a balance sheet. It is interesting to note that when Nestle bought Rowntree (chocolates) in the UK in a multi-million pound deal, barely 20 per cent was for the value of tangible plant machinery and assets and over 80 per cent was for brand goodwill—or the value of the relationship that the Rowntree brands enjoyed with the British!

Recognizing the importance of consumer and customer goodwill, some companies have gone to the extent of documenting that a 'right side up' company is an inverted pyramid with those that are closest to the customer interaction having the greatest empowerment. Such a company is driven more by what the consumer wants than what the Chief Executive Officer (CEO) dictates. The focus of the top and middle management is to facilitate the performance of their roles by those in the frontline of customer interaction. Taken to its logical conclusion, this means empowerment not only of the frontline staff dealing with customers (dealers) but rather the training and development of those dealers themselves so that they can better service their (and the company's) final consumers.

Customer orientation has increased in every company to a greater or lesser degree but the need is to accelerate it. Why?

Spiralling Competition

During the licence *raj*, business success depended more on obtaining the manufacturer's licence than on winning customers. With a two-year wait-list for a Bajaj scooter, a 'premium' on the Maruti and a year-long wait-list for a telephone connection, the consumer was hardly the 'king'. Rather, it was a supplier's market and poor Mr Sharma had to use 'connections' to even get the cement bags he wanted to use to construct his house, or pay a premium. Did customer relations matter in such an environment?

Not surprisingly, during that period, the consumer was a poor 'beggar', lucky to have received the goods he had paid for, while warranties expired on the payment of the invoice and service was virtually unknown for the vast majority of products and services. Small wonder then was the growing craze for 'phoren' goods, the poor quality of Indian merchandise and Indian goods which invariably were unable to compete in the world markets.

The dismantling of government controls and deregulation/liberalization of the 1990s have changed the scenario dramatically. For instance, with newer cars, Maruti saw its market share erode by over 20 per cent and is wooing customers with discounts, free gifts, better after-sales service and a customer satisfaction campaign. It is interesting to note that a former public sector company is the one which is focusing on customer satisfaction (as shown by customer satisfaction surveys) as the major reason to buy a Maruti car. Is your company in a position to make a similar claim?

Indian Airlines has also introduced a frequent flyer programme and apex fares, as well as a choice of menus in business class. It had better. Else the consumer will choose to fly Jet Airways or Sahara Airlines.

Similarly, for years, Kelvinator refrigerator was 'the coolest one' and there were few other brands. Now there are LG, Samsung, Electrolux, Godrej, Whirlpool and White Westinghouse, amongst others. The customer now has a choice and will be respected for it.

The competition for the consumer's spend has further increased with the reduction of import barriers. For example, there is not only Amul,Verka and Britannia cheese, there is also legally imported Kraft and Laughing Cow. Indian goods must compete freely in India with goods from all over the world including China, as bicycle manufacturers have realized. Winning and retaining customers is not a choice—it is a matter of survival.

Spiralling competition is a trend that will only increase in the next few years as India integrates itself further with the world economy, and the World Trade Organization (WTO) makes the global village a reality, and newer and more products hit the market.

Look at the furniture that is coming in from the Far East and Europe. Today, the Indian consumer can choose whether to opt for one or the other, or buy an Indian brand, or even depend, as in the not-so-distant past, upon the neighbourhood carpenter. With India's foreign exchange reserve burgeoning and exports growing in spite of an appreciating rupee, and with growing trade links with even China and Pakistan, the future for 'consumer choice' is mind boggling.

The choice becomes even greater when one considers the liberalization of the foreign-exchange controls. A resident Indian can now remit up to US$ 25,000 per calendar year without assigning any reasons or taking any permissions. This means Mr Rama can choose to take his family for a holiday to Goa or to Phuket, Thailand, or any other holiday destination abroad. He can even buy on installment through a mortgage, a property in Greater London, rather than a flat in Mumbai. Goods can be bought through the Internet using an international credit card. So your choice is restricted only by the amount of rupees you have and are willing to spend or borrow! There are hardly any supply-side restrictions with customs duties also a fraction of what they were a few years ago.

Some Points to Ponder

- ❏ How many models of cars were available five years ago, how many are available today and how many are expected five years from now?
- ❏ How many products are being marketed in your industry today? What about five years ago and five years later?
- ❏ How many phone services were there five years ago and how many are there now?
- ❏ What is the basic consumer need you are fulfilling? Is it a need, comfort, or luxury for the industry and for your brand?
- ❏ What are the various uses of your product? What generic competitor is there for each of these types of usages?
- ❏ What is the reason for the non-usage of your company's products i.e., a shrinkage of your industry size?

The Fragmentation of Media

TV was introduced in India in 1959 and went colour 20 years later. Then, for about a decade, advertisers could reach a national audience through the only national channel which was government owned—Doordarshan. In the 1990s, the 'cable' revolution began and fed 20 private satellite channels overnight into Indian homes. It was more difficult to achieve advertising reach because with choice, one programme seldom attracts the kind of mass audience that a *Mahabharat* or a Hindi feature film did in the past.

Today, TV channels deliver content in all major Indian languages, reflecting both greater CRM (speaking the customer's language) and greater difficulty/cost for advertisers. Advertisers need to know what their consumers are watching in great detail—making media planning more specialized, especially when one considers that the medium is also a message (for example, a Hindi ad in a Tamil movie!).

The print scenario is no different, with a multitude of covers for various audiences and the emergence of specialist magazines. Similarly, radio channels have multiplied with the advent of FM. Some of the most popular channels did not even exist a year ago—like Radio Mirchi—and by next year there will be other new ones.

Completely new media has also come into existence—the short messaging service or SMS over mobile phones. Currently, mobile service providers do not allow it to be used for broadcasting anything but their own promotional messages. However, this medium is becoming increasingly popular for promotional purposes like contests, where the consumer has to send an SMS. In 2005, the number of cellular subscribers in India (industry data) is expected to exceed landlines. This means that there will be more people who could be SMSed than reached by all the newspapers put together. The potential power of the new medium! Indeed, the cell phone has already become an advertising medium to deliver personalized messages. During the recent Lok Sabha elections, you may have personally received a call from the former Prime Minister, Atal Bihari Vajpayee on your cell phone (as did many others) in what was a unique a one-to-one marketing effort by the Bharatiya Janata Party (BJP). The power of technology has fragmented the media like never before.

To appreciate the potential of the mobile phone, one need only consider the fact that in Delhi there are already more cellular phones than landlines, and whereas in India in 2001, cell subscribers were 14 per cent of the total, in China they were 44 per cent, in the US 44 per cent, the UK 57 per cent, Singapore 60 per cent, Philippines 78 per cent and Bangladesh 47 per cent (TCS, 2003–04)!

The consumer also has the choice of media over the Internet. Although the dotcom boom went bust rather quickly and Internet connections in India in the non-business world are still limited to the upper fringes of society, there is no denying that the Internet will steadily grow in popularity and is another 'media' possibility. For example, naukri.com competes effectively with the newspapers for job vacancies. Indeed, in some cases where fulfillment is required, the Internet is more effective. For example, rediff.com and Indiatimes.com are two very effective channels for the advertisement and sale of books, flowers and other merchandise, and they can specifically reach those of their users who are interested in them. Like the SMS, they can be used for one-to-one marketing in a cost-effective way.

It is very important to appreciate that both the SMS and the Internet are highly personalized media. They allow for one-to-one marketing and, in fact, individualized mass marketing. Since the medium is also a message and over half of India's population is less than 25 years old, the SMS and Internet are, no doubt, growing and important mediums of advertising in the future.

Some Points to Ponder

- ❑ How many TV channels existed five years ago, how many are there today and how many do you think there will be five years from now?
- ❑ What is the future of FM radio?
- ❑ Name some of the magazines that your home subscribes to. Who reads each magazine?
- ❑ When did you first use the SMS, and when did you first participate in an SMS contest or activity?
- ❑ How often do you go to a website to find out more information? Do you think this will become an increasing trend?

To remain connected with their target audience, marketers must know them better and define them more precisely. The shotgun approach, with the target audience definition merely being 'households with a monthly family income of Rs 1500 plus', is no longer enough.

You need to know what the customer reads, which channels he/she watches and listens to and where does he/she hang out. Knowledge is power, else the limited

media and promotional budget will be wasted or at best, inefficiently spent.

Rise of Individualism

The breakdown of the joint family system and increase of nuclear families is well known. What is becoming increasingly evident is greater individualism with greater affluence and double income families—multiple TV ownership, for example. He watches cricket while she watches films—not necessarily on 'picture-in-picture' (PIP).

With the increase in the number of career women, the incidence of husband and wife living in different cities is also increasing, as are the cases of more than one home (a farmhouse) in the same city due to greater affluence. Time pressures means more material goods for the children and an increasingly 'me' focused society. This is not necessarily in a negative way but factually, the multiple ownership of various goods and services proves it particularly in urban areas and the larger metropolises like Delhi and Mumbai.

In a *Businessworld* survey (*Businessworld*, 6 October 2003) conducted by NFO MBL India, over 9 per cent of the respondents in Delhi indicated that they were planning to buy a second colour TV or fridge, and 1.8 per cent even said they intended to buy a second washing machine. These are not replacement buying but additional purchases.

Again, perhaps nothing symbolizes the rise of individualism more than the mobile phone. How many households have two, or even three phones, each different from the other? Compare the situation with just a few years ago, where there was one rotary black instrument provided by MTNL or BSNL, with one ringing tone across the country for every phone. That phone connection was at best placed in many rooms but access to the phone was common and there was probably one common family address book. Cut to today's mobile. Available in a price range from Rs 3,000 a set to over Rs 30,000. With a choice of 15–20 ring tones built in—which you can change from time-to-time in a matter of seconds, or personalize them for individuals or groups. And if you are not happy with what you got built in—for a few rupees more you can download them on your screen and if you are not happy with that, you can download Madhuri Dixit's pretty face via SMS and stare into it every time you first look at your cell phone! And your ring tone and wallpaper will be different for you and your wife because she, in all likelihood, has her own mobile. But if she does not, she can change Madhuri to Ajay Devgan and hear her preferred tones when she is using the common phone!

Consumers have a relationship with products they use particularly if they use them often and it is this relationship that marketers need to nurture in an increasingly competitive and individualized world. Again, consider the mobile phone and the multitude of choices available in the market and how mobile companies are making the phone an integral part of an individual's life by personalizing it. Hutch launched a new series of numbers where the advertising theme was that you could make your wedding date or your birthday your mobile number. Hutch also launched a pizza service for its pre-paid consumers, where they can choose special price plans like SMS at 60 p, for friends and family and change these on a weekly basis themselves! All this just by sending an SMS.

The rise of individualism has also been fuelled by greater westernization and modernization. As affluence grows and Indians are more exposed to the relatively more individualized society of the West, 'me' becomes more important. The Hindu joint family is fast fading away even in the smaller towns and villages.

The rise of individualism can also be attributed to the greater desire for material wealth and possessions as in the West. There are more goods to desire, much more choice and more media to fan you to desire them. So, the 'I want' factor is growing.

With the majority of the Indian population under 25, there has never been a generation more exposed to the West or the TV, more educated and more liberated. This is only going to grow as India becomes more developed and exposed to the world through greater trade and tourism.

Some Points to Ponder

- ❑ Has the number of single homes you know increased or decreased vs five years ago?
- ❑ Do you know a greater number of two-car households now than five years ago, and do you think this number will increase with time?
- ❑ Do you think there are a greater number of mobile owners today with more than one phone in the same household? What about five years from now?
- ❑ Do you know of families which have lived in different cities for long periods of time due to career needs?

Technological Advances

Technological advances are now leading to Adam Smith's 'pure competition'. Take the share market. There was a time when share brokers charged 1–2 per cent commission for transactions in the stock exchange of the same city, and 3–4 per cent for transactions in the stock exchange of another city. There was also the possibility of playing on the actual price transacted and that quoted to the client. Now with the National Stock Exchange (NSE) and computerized national trading, broking rates are down to a quarter of 1 per cent or less, and there is one national market. It is even possible to directly trade yourself like by registering with kotakstreet.com. The speed of transactions has also multiplied manifold. From a situation where it took almost a 15–30 days to consummate a share transaction, this is done now in a matter of three days, especially since shares have been dematerialized—become records on computers rather than share certificates and transfer deeds. Technological advances have meant not only greater speed in transactions and transparency but a different role for the broker. Excellence and speed in service is necessary to survive, and to thrive, he needs to build strong relationships with his customers because there is little to choose in 'rates' and 'transparency' between one broker and another.

Similarly, the travel agent must provide excellent service to his clients because information is available on the net and the principal (the airlines) are competing directly through the Internet. Almost all airlines and hotels/resorts today have their own websites. So, the Internet savvy consumer has a choice of booking directly or through the travel agent, and the airline/hotel has the choice of passing on some of the agents' commission to conclude the deal. As the popularity of the Internet grows, the travel agent must depend upon his knowledge of his customers to be able to quickly personalize the offering to them vs an all-encompassing but more impersonal Internet, and also develop a relationship with them where they prefer to deal with him than do the booking themselves.

Another technological advance—the remote— makes escaping advertising messages easy by allowing channel surfing. So, if an advertisement does not inform or entertain it will simply be 'zapped'. It would be an interesting exercise for marketers to do a quick estimate of what percentage of their ads are zapped or actually seen and, therefore, what is the real Opportunity to See (OTS) and actual cost per thousand.

The Conditional Access System (CAS) will eventually happen. When it does, TV channels must deliver or they will simply not be watched. The extent of penetration of a particular channel will be quantified and known. Revenues will flow from that, as popularity can determine subscription rates and, of course, ad rates as well. The consumer vote will become a durable whammy.

Broadband will allow for video-on-demand and one can choose the movie he/she sees on the movie channel rather than see what the cable operator chooses to relay.

CD ROMs allow for interaction and can be films, games, music, art, catalogues or reference sources. So, there is greater consumer involvement than in the passive participation of traditional TV or video.

You can also design your own newspaper—only news about Indian politics and cricket, for example, or just films. Most publications are now on the net.

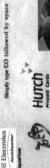

The mobile phone is a technological advance that information providers have to contend with. For example, stock prices are available ex SMS as is the weather and political news. Hutch has launched a service where you SMS Dial4pizza and the address of the nearest Dominos Pizza outlet will be SMSed back to you. You can use the mobile phone to access chocolate from a Cadbury's dispenser in Bombay and the amount will be charged to your cell bill!! If it works, this opens up the possibility of a new mode of payment collection and overcomes the problem of change in dispensing machines.

Some Points to Ponder

- Go to the *India Today* website at www.Indiatoday.com. What choices do you have? What does it imply for the traditional magazine trade?
- Go to www.rediff.com and see how you can choose and order different products directly on the net.
- Go to www.kotakstreet.com and try and visualize how you would place a financial services ad.

Realization that Existing Customers are Important

Businesses typically spend five times as much money getting new customers than retaining existing ones. But there is a growing realization that customer retention is easier and more profitable.

A satisfied consumer tells 3–5 other people of his experience. A delighted consumer is one who finds that what is delivered is more than what is promised/expected. A dissatisfied consumer not only stops consuming your product but tells nine or 10 other people about his experience. So, if you calculate the 'life-time value of this satisfaction/dissatisfaction', you will see the real impact of a brand switch. For example, a 20-year-old consuming one tube of toothpaste a month will consume $12 \times 50 = 600$ tubes during his lifetime. Therefore, if he is dissatisfied and switches brands, what could Colgate lose directly in terms of its sales? And possibly in terms of his friends and relatives' sales as well?

This sort of situation occurs in the case of consumer durables as well. You may think that you have sold your customer an air conditioner which will last for 15 years. What can the 'poor chap' do now? Well, the 'poor chap' need not buy your brand when he buys his next few air conditioners. If he is really unhappy, he will talk about his unhappiness and this could persuade others not to buy your brand. Conversely, if he is really happy with your product he will be a brand champion and this could influence others into also buying it. We all know how important word of mouth is for expensive purchases, be they cars, or household appliances.

Given in this chapter is a schematic representation of the purchase decision. Think about how important word of mouth is and how customer friendly is your company.

Do the following questionnaire to decide whether you need and want to do more for CRM in your organization.

If the competition is scoring higher on these customer-relationship scores, which brand do you think the

1. Serving our customers' needs takes precedence over serving our internal needs.
2. We do not make promises to customers we know we cannot deliver.
3. We use information from customers to design or improve our products or services.
4. We welcome complaints from customers.
5. We promptly reply to consumer complaints.
6. We provide opportunities for employees from all levels and departments regularly to meet customers.
7. We regularly ask customers to give us feedback about our performance.
8. Our key managers clearly understand and broadcast the needs of our customers.
9. Our employees at all levels are encouraged and empowered to exceed customers' expectations.
10. We try to resolve all complaints to the complete delight of our customers.
11. Consumers have directly contributed to new products/ packs/promotional strategy or plans.

(Contd.)

(*Contd.*)

12. Consumers with problems can quickly and conveniently contact us through various mediums—phones, SMS, email/regular mail.

consumer will buy? As product and price differentials narrow, information is more completely and readily available, and as the consumer has the choice of deciding and placing the order in his own home via the Internet, the role of 'relationship' becomes greater. Given the environmental factors at play, is there really any choice other than focusing on delighting the consumer? The road to customer delight—the TINA factor—**T**here **I**s **N**o **A**lternative! Lets travel it with enthusiasm.

Do Not Forget Internal Customers

While the need for being externally focused and customer delight has never been greater, you can afford to ignore your internal customers only at your peril.

Sales and profits in the long run can only be achieved by a corporation which seeks to stretch the envelope for customer delight just beyond its own past offering and that of competition but with financial and operational discipline.

We believe a truly right side up company is not an inverted pyramid but a set of interlinked, inverted functional three-dimensional pyramids or prisms.

The rainbow can be seen only after light (corporate energy) passes through the prism.

Let us look at some of the inter-connectivities.

If marketing wants more information about consumer purchase habits this can be done by the sales team collecting the data and the IT team collating and processing it in a form and format mutually agreed upon by all three teams. If this is not agreed to, or if the sales team does not collect it, or IT process it as required, marketing cannot have the insight to try and develop a strategy to delight the consumer.

Take sales and operations—sales for customer delight will require a number of SKUs—virtually, the more the merrier. But this will not only create a problem for them in terms of selling, it will create operational problems in terms of production scheduling, small production runs, multiple inventories and the greater likelihood of stock outs of individual units, not to mention higher operational costs and lower profits. So, external customer delight must be measured and balanced with internal customers to delight the consumers.

Take marketing, operations and personnel—if marketing were to strategically decide to start selling highly labour-intensive products made by many relatively low-skilled workers in a company, which has traditionally sold high-value products made by highly-automated processes manned by few highly-paid workers, or vice versa, this is going to have an impact on the company culture, employee relations and programmes. This, in turn, would impact the company's actual delivery on the customer expectation score card, both in terms of type of products expected and also quality of products expected. It would change not only the benchmarks within the company but also the benchmarks in the eyes of the customer.

Another case between marketing and sales. In order to delight the customer with a 10 per cent lower price while maintaining the needs of the internal finance consumer, the marketing group of a hotel could propose a disintermediation process, where sales would only be directly through the net, thereby saving the agents' commission. But while this would give a marketing advantage, it would reduce service levels as far as distribution points and could not only reduce customer satisfaction but result in actual lost sales because the customer, for example, does not use the net, or only likes making his travel bookings through a particular agent.

Just like a good salary structure, a company's customer delight offering must be externally competitive *and* internally equitable. To use terminology from the Myers Brigg-type indicator: *the chosen solution must be externally driven—by competition and customer and internally balanced between the chemistry and needs of the body corporate.*

Points to Remember

It is important to get to know your customer better and develop a strong relationship with him because of:

- Greater competition (including imports, thanks to the WTO) leading to greater consumer choice.
- Fragmentation of media and new media.
- Rise of individualism—the 'me' generation.
- Technological advances, particularly the cellular phone (SMS) and the Internet. All these trends

are likely to accentuate in the future, making better CRM even more imperative.

- Existing customers are potential customers of the future and their opinion and usage has a multiplier effect especially when one considers the 'lifetime value'.

However, it is equally important to understand and appreciate the needs of internal customers. They too have external customers. For example, if pricing is done on the basis of delighting the customer, it could bankrupt the company. If too long a credit period is given, there could be a liquidity crunch resulting in a delay in salary payment resulting in employee attrition, resulting in problems in execution. So, external customer needs on price and credit have to be balanced with internal finance needs. Similarly, product quality and delivery schedule 'delight' has to be balanced with internal production. A balance between the two is required for sustained customer delight. So, the key is to strive for sustainable customer delight and a growing share of wallet and loyalty.

Chapter 2

Taking an Integrated Approach

TRADITIONAL marketing has essentially been mass marketing—based on the economies of scale of mass production and mass media. Competition, resulting in greater segmentation, media fragmentation and the information age, has resulted in a paradigm shift—the breakdown of the critical mass. The manufacturer no longer controls the relationship. This has largely happened in the West and will happen in India as well.

So, there needs to be a stronger relationship. This can be achieved by:

- ◆ adding value to a product (like serving suggestions to a culinary aid);
- ◆ values (like the prestige of driving a Mercedes);
- ◆ through more intimate consumer contact; or
- ◆ treating products like service brands.

But most importantly, there needs to be consistency across the various elements of the marketing mix so that the consumer gets the 'same message' from different channels which would result in synergy.

In the mid-1980s, Nestle's Milkmaid Sweetened Condensed Milk was used as a whitener. Volumes were dropping rapidly due to the greater availability of powder and liquid milk. It was decided to reposition the product as a culinary ingredient, so all elements of the marketing mix were brought in line. The plain white label was changed to have a third of the tin covered with an attractive photograph of a dessert (with the simple recipe on the reverse). Consumer promotions were near packs (related to lead recipes) like *kulfi* moulds and *seviyan.* An offer of a free colour recipe booklet (bilingual) was made in all communication—packs and media—and the booklet was promptly dispatched to all the 10,000 people who wrote in every month. All media was naturally dessert-recipe related. A *Milkmaid Gold Collection* of 101 recipes was published to further consolidate the positioning. A distribution drive was launched amongst bakeries and non-traditional outlets.

Sales decline was dramatically reversed, even though prices were increased. This occurred because all the 'messages' to the consumer were the same—Milkmaid makes tasty desserts quickly and conveniently. It is interesting that initially the desserts promoted were Western ones like flan and meringue. But when research showed that consumers preferred the desserts they were familiar with and were looking for quick recipes with few readily available ingredients, Indian desserts were incorporated.

Some Points to Ponder

- ❏ Think of an example where a brand followed a total integrated approach. What were the sales results?
- ❏ Think of a brand in your company, or any other for that matter, and closely examine what elements in the total customer experience are inconsistent with the stated positioning and what should be done to change this.
- ❏ What new innovative programmes has Hindustan Lever and L'Oreal launched to promote its 'beauty' products—branded or franchised beauty parlours and hair dressing salons!

Traditionally, there were four Ps—Product (including packaging), Price, Promotion and Place. To these we now need to add another four—Positioning, Passion, People and Personality. The first four Ps were 'objective'. The new four Ps are subjective—what we feel. All must be in concert for best results.

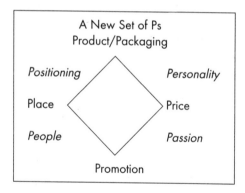

A New Set of Ps
Product/Packaging
Positioning
Personality
Place
Price
People
Passion
Promotion

You will agree that we act based not only on what *we think* but what *we feel*. In fact, at least sometimes, what we feel overwhelms what we think. Take colas, for example. Aerated black water—and the young feel passionately about it because of the 'total experience' Pepsi and Coke deliver—both physical (cooling thirst) and emotional (identification with the stars and cricketers and other youth). Sometimes a controversy like the pesticide residue issue gets the 'thinking' public to overwhelm the emotional but once the controversy was resolved, sales bounced back and the emotional connection was re-established.

It is important to decide on what primary platform the brand is to be based—thought or emotions. Ideally, both should complement each other. If you are using thinking as the main primer, it helps to take the moral high ground by educating consumers about their needs and benefits in a generic manner. Insurance companies and financial companies do this as well as OTC drug brands.

On the other hand, if you are using emotion, a great way to reflect that is humour, as Pepsi does so brilliantly, or fear as many of the OTC brands or government enforcement agencies do. The success of the latter is, of course, dependent upon the reality check and actual consumer experience and word of mouth. A fear campaign of a hefty fine or impoundment of your car will not work if in reality the enforcing policeman can be 'managed'.

In addition to the TV advertisement, promotions and distribution must also spread the same message to the consumers. It is important for people in the company to also do this—at least those interacting directly with the consumers. For example, the reputation and image of a hospital is determined not only by the quality of its doctors and nurses but also by the way the call-centre executives handle calls to the hospital. In fact, in many cases before a patient visits a hospital, he first calls it and if his query is not fielded politely and efficiently, he may well decide not to visit the hospital at all. It is amazing that at one of India's premier hospitals that was researched, it took almost two minutes to be able to get through the emergency section and requests for information were often passed from extension to extension. The call-centre executives did not use pleasantries like 'thank you' and 'please' and were clearly in a hurry to transfer the call to an extension where, often, there was no person to answer and they would not even check if there was anyone to handle the call! Is this consistent with the hospitals' desired positioning of an institution, which displays tender loving care? Should the call centre or reception of a premier hospital be in any way not at least as caring as that of a star hotel?

Viewed conceptually, all product attributes and activities are linked, and from the composite whole a consumer forms his relationship with the product, be it positioning, usage or advocacy.

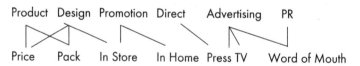

The need, therefore, is consistency:

♦ one strategy;
♦ across all media;
♦ dynamic not static;

- as media merge;
- not marketing vs sales;
- not tactics vs strategy.

This should be the same message across everything, everywhere, all the time. It involves owning the customer relationship:

- across time;
- across media;
- across technology;
- across borders;
- by re-engineering where necessary.

Total Band Integration: 'band' management more than brand management, or specialists playing in concert.

Here is a literal example of Band Marketing: Yanni, the composer/musician:

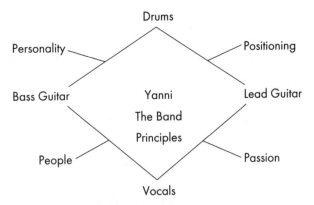

The sum was greater than the parts—*Yanni Live at the Acropolis*; *Yanni Live at Agra*. Look at the offering—a band consisting of musicians from many different countries with different instruments performing at different wonders of the world (mute spectators to history). Would the music have sounded the same had it not been performed live at the Acropolis and with the Taj as the background? Would our listening pleasure have been the same or would the sales of the CDs have been the same without the controversy and historical setting to the music?

Consider:

The Band Brand Miracle	
• The Musicians	• The Merchandise
• The Music	• The Tour
• The Album Sleeve	• The T-shirt
• The Performance	• The CD ROM
• The Video	• The PR
• The Logo	

The synergy creates the legend—the larger than life image.

Similarly, would Bollywood be the same without star gossip and magazines like *Stardust, Movie* and *Showtime*? They enjoy a symbiotic relationship, as does the sponsorship and commercialization of cricket in India. Would cricket be the same if the cricketers were not brand ambassadors for so many brands and part of our everyday lives—be it refrigerators, soft drinks, TVs, cars, motorcycles or shaving cream!

The advertising medium chosen also conveys a message. The medium is the message. Consider a short message and think about whether it would have a different meaning if conveyed by traditional mail (post), SMS, a landline, or a mobile phone. How intrusive should you and do you want to be? It is important that this integration be done across geographical boundaries too.

The world is increasingly becoming a global village. While there will need to be differences between countries like say left-hand drive and right-hand drive for cars, or the chilli level in food, or bitterness in beer, nonetheless, the overall proposition for a brand must be the same in all countries.

People travel and media is increasingly becoming international too. With the WTO trade barriers coming down, world trade is bound to grow exponentially. It is also becoming important for advertising, given the amount there is to 'stand on its own feet'—that is, either educate the consumer or entertain him. Two examples of entertaining press campaigns are at the end of this chapter. As one wag put it, 'sometimes one has to go through a lot of boring programmes to see a good commercial'. Advertising must delight or at least 'attempt' to and reach partly there or be zapped/tuned out.

Some Points to Ponder

- ❏ Think of two examples where a product successfully followed a holistic approach.
- ❏ Why did Coke have to quickly launch Coke Classic?
- ❏ What new services has Maruti launched?
- ❏ What services does ICICI and HDFC Home Loans offer in addition to Home Loans?

Every Interaction Matters

One instance of consumer delight can do more for building a relationship with a brand than years of advertising.

Look at it this way.
You didn't lose a bottle of Chivas;
you gained a few friends.

"You're some tomato.
We could make beautiful Bloody Marys together.
I'm different from those other fellows."

"I like you, Wolfschmidt.
You've got taste."

Wolfschmidt Vodka has the touch of taste that marks genuine old world vodka. Wolfschmidt in a Bloody Mary is a tomato in triumph.Wolfschmidt brings out the best in every drink. General Wine and Spirits Company, N.Y. 22. Made from Grain, 80 or 100 Proof. Prod. of U.S.A.

For example, I had secured enough points in the Swissair Qualifyer programme to earn a free weekend stay at the Swissotel at Brussels. When I checked into the hotel, not only was I made to feel special (although I was a non-paying guest) but we were upgraded to an executive suite, where breakfast and drinks in the evening were on the house. I have flown many airlines and had many experiences but somehow I would still rate Swissair the best and given a choice fly that airline (it now exists under a different brand name—SWISS International Air Lines).

Contrast that with some airlines, where points lapse after a certain time period if you do not cash them—often without warning! Or you can fly subject to availability, which tends to give you a contradictory message: you are special because you fly so often with us and we would like to thank you for your custom but actually you are also our least priority customer and can only get on if the seat is empty! Thankfully, this is not common practice but I have known cases where Gold members (the highest category of frequent flyers with the airline) have been offloaded when they are flying on a free ticket!

Similarly, one bad experience with your brand or company will mean that the consumer has a negative attitude towards your other offerings as well. Jupiter Research's recent study found that 70 per cent of about 2,000 American shoppers decided to spend less money in a retailer's brick operation if they were dissatisfied with the clicks experience (www.crmguru.com). There is a saying that goes: 'You (being what you are) speak so loud that I cannot hear what you say'.

You are lucky if the consumer decided to complain—at least it gives you the chance to rectify the problem. In over 90 per cent of the cases, consumers simply change brands. So, it is important to enable consumers to reach the company (set up helplines, talk to customers at random, visit trade and consumers as often as you can) and research consumer behaviour/get feedback as much as possible. Consider yourself as a consumer of your company's product and think of what you would need to do if you had a problem. Better still, test it out and perhaps you will be chastised and surprised by the experience.

An interaction can cause you to win or lose a customer. Calculate the life-time value of the consumer (unit consumption × expected consumption in a year × consumers life expectancy) and you will see how important each transaction and interaction with the consumer is. Keep him/her satisfied. It is far easier and far more profitable to retain a customer than to acquire a new one. Yet, many businesses today take the existing consumer for granted while lavishing attention and expense on trying to get a new one.

Imagine the life-time value of a consumer as a number he carried on his/her forehead. Accordingly, if a grocer saw a housewife with a number as Rs 2,000 per month×12 mths×50 years=Rs 120,000, won't he treat her with a bit more care if she asked to replace or return a bottle of jam she had bought by mistake?

Similarly, if the Machino Techno Maruti car dealership realized that a consumer probably buys 10–20 cars during his lifetime then would they not happily arrange to pick up and drop the car for service, send birthday and anniversary cards or perhaps even a small gift and generally show they are glad for his custom? An excellent example of how a car dealership can be run profitability through the principle of customer delight is in the

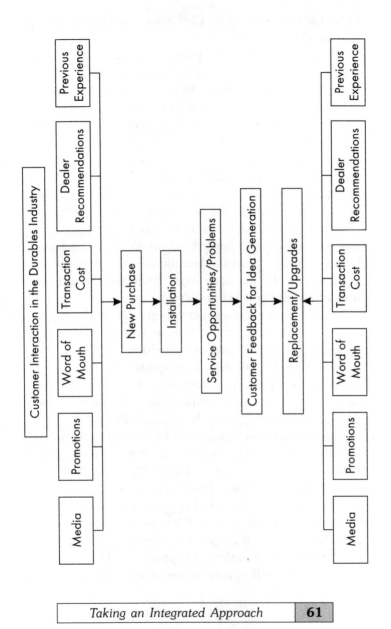

Customer Interaction in the Durables Industry

Media — Promotions — Word of Mouth — Transaction Cost — Dealer Recommendations — Previous Experience

New Purchase → Installation → Service Opportunities/Problems → Customer Feedback for Idea Generation → Replacement/Upgrades

Media — Promotions — Word of Mouth — Transaction Cost — Dealer Recommendations — Previous Experience book *Customers for Life* by Carl Sewell and Paul B. Brown (Pocket Books, 1998).

The examples and practice of customer delight would do well in the consumer durable industry in India. Murphy's law really holds true—all warranties lapse on payment of invoice. The companies forget that the 'poor' consumer may not be able to do anything about the washing machine or fridge that he has bought and have to put up with all the suffering that is inflicted upon him for parting with his hard-earned money. But he can and will tell many of his friends and relatives and also not choose to buy your product the next time he buys other consumer durables, or even a second fridge or washing machine a few years later. A schematic representation of how a customer makes a decision on consumer durables is shown on the previous page. Reflection would show how important goodwill is.

Look at our homes. Do you give as much attention and importance to your spouse as you do to a new acquaintance you are trying to make friends with, or is your spouse taken for granted. Your spouse is your customer too as are your children and your old friends and business associates. Every transaction with them matters, though fortunately, given the multiplicity and frequency of transactions, an occasional bloomer or problem is quickly forgotten. That is because there is enough equity in the relationship—enough bank balance to draw from.

Similarly, in the relationship between your brand and the consumer, try and build and consolidate equity. Even if you are in a leadership position, surprise the customer with a gift or give him/her some special attention which he will notice and appreciate. This is particularly true in B2B relationships. One rude remark or discourtesy, or taking the consumer for granted can destroy millions of rupees worth of business.

So, can taking the consumer for granted seriously impact market shares. Do not mess round with the consumer! J. Sainsbury was the leading grocery multiple in the UK, until they increasingly decided to mainly stock the Sainsbury brand in their stores and use the consumer preference for the store to restrict his choice. The result is that Tesco, which continued to have a good balance between brands and their private label, is now the market leader. And Sainsbury has lost the brand and the private label leadership, as well as lots of revenue and profit.

Customers and Consumer Goodwill

It is important to realize that in these competitive times, customer or trade (distributor, wholesaler, retailer) goodwill is important because it is they who provide the final interface with the ultimate consumer.

In India in the past, due to the suppliers' market and fragmentation of trade, marketers tended to take the trade for granted. Retailers operated at under 10 per cent gross margin for fast moving consumer goods (FMCG) products and barely 2–3 per cent net of discount margin or consumer durables. Distributors were subjected to 'dumping'—stock selling and inventories in excess of agreed norms. Retailers were not skilled or sophisticated in inventory or space management and so could be persuaded to act against their best interests by salesmen, which they often were.

Things have changed dramatically in the last few years due to the increase in product offerings, greater awareness amongst retailers, the growth of organized trade in India and some of the more enlightened business houses seeking to increase efforts in winning trade goodwill and service levels—for example, free distribution of visi-coolers (fridges) by Pepsi and Coke on a select basis.

Some brands, realizing the importance of retailing, have set up their own retail shops—Hutch and Airtel cellular services and Arrow Garments, Titan Watches, LG and Sony—besides being present in multi-brand ones. This trend of having own branded outlets is likely to accentuate in the future, both across brands and across territories for brands—so the more the brands, the more the outlets.

Another trend is the linking of individual retail outlets (chemists, grocers, convenience stores and STD booths) electronically for payment purposes. This has been done for lotteries by the Apollo (Tyre) Group (Lotus games) and for payment of utility bills by customers by Easy Bill (a Hero Honda or Munjal Group Company). In the latter case, the company seeks to delight both customers (retailers) and consumers. For a small fee (Rs 5–10), the consumers have the choice of paying their utility bills at any of the Easy Bill outlets which are electronically linked (like credit cards) to the Easy Bill hub, which give them a final receipt on the spot. The consumer has the convenience; the retailer, the benefit of additional foot falls and regular custom, besides a better stature within his local market. Easy Bill has also guaranteed each of its franchisees, from whom they take a Rs 50,000 security deposit for the EPOS machine, a certain minimum revenue per month. And if during the initial period there is a shortfall, they top it up!

Another trend prevalent particularly in the metros, is the development of malls like the best of those abroad.

Glitzy, and with multiple offerings, restaurants and movie halls, these malls will change the way many Indians shop and they definitely will change the way goods are merchandised, displayed and sold. It is not difficult to imagine a 'mall' loyalty programme where points are earned by the amount you spend across different stores in a mall, as malls compete to delight the customer and the stakes could be half a day's shopping plus a movie plus dinner!

'Direct to home' services are also likely to grow as consumers become comfortable ordering on the Internet using credit cards and by using the phone. Tickets to Indian Railways, once only available through serpentine queues, can now be purchased over the Internet. Most restaurants have free home delivery through phone within a specified radius. You can make a list of greeting cards you want to buy and for a small fee, Archies will send them for you. You only need to ring up the concierge of your building and they will send you a carpenter, plumber or electrician besides flowers, and speciality foods. Customer convenience has arrived, at least in the metros of India.

But while all these new formats will grow—exclusive branded outlets, franchisees, malls, direct to home and new ones like speciality stores will come up, it will be many years yet before one can write off the traditional retailer in any channel—be it FMCG, consumer durables or financial services. The latter have strong personalized links and personalized knowledge, and while not being as sophisticated and often even so educated as their more 'professional' brethren, nonetheless, their services borne out of sheer experience and 'doing it' themselves, is often hard to beat.

The challenge is to choose the customers (trade) and service level for each product (SKU) so as to best be able to delight the customer as well as the final consumer. And do it in a manner where each element of the distribution, depth and width compliments each other.

Some Points to Ponder

- ❏ Think of any interaction which comes first to mind when you think of exceptional service from a hotel. What is your overall attitude towards that hotel?
- ❏ Think of what you feel about a bank whose telecallers keep calling you at all times to buy a credit card.
- ❏ Think about how you can make a more synergestic offering to your customer across all eight elements of the marketing mix.
- ❏ Think about how you can have special transactions (customer delight that decisively builds brand equity with your consumers—your clients, consumers and your key family members and colleagues).

Points to Remember

- • Mass marketing is becoming less effective.
- • We need to understand our customers well.
- • Speak to the consumer in terms and language he can relate to.
- • Customer relationships are built by the sum of all the experiences he has with the brand. So, it is important to have consistency in your approach.
- • Customer relationships are built not only by what a consumer thinks (Product, Price, Packaging,

Promotion, Place) but what he feels (Product positioning, Interaction with company people and his own personality).

- Different distribution channels exist and more will come up. The right width and depth have to be decided for each stock keeping unit of each product bearing customer, consumer and company interests in mind.

- Each and every interaction with the consumer is important since it has a multiplier effect. Try and 'delight' him whenever you can—one interaction could be worth more than many thousands of rupees of mass marketing.

Chapter 3

Database Management

To build a good relationship with someone necessarily requires knowing him/her well—the better you know your customer, the better you can try and meet his/her needs. CRM, therefore, involves database management as well. This becomes even more important when the 'mass market' breaks down to an individualistic one. Databases can be acquired through many means. Some of these are discussed below.

Bar Coding

Bar coding and technology have made the compilation of detailed purchasing behaviour practicable. There are two types of bar codes—ITF and EAN and what they look like, and what the bars stand for, is shown in the following pages.

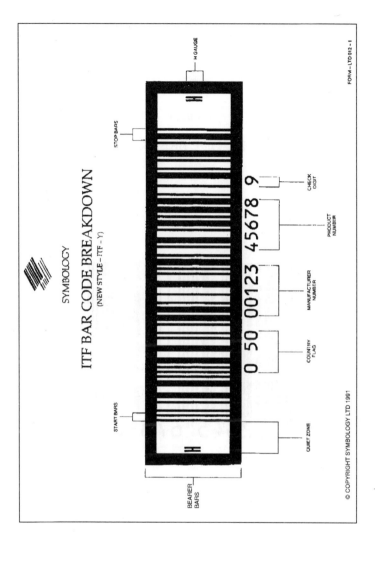

SYMBOLOGY

ITF BAR CODE BREAKDOWN
(NEW STYLE - ITF - Y)

H GAUGE

STOP BARS

CHECK
DIGIT

9

45678

PRODUCT
NUMBER

00123

MANUFACTURER
NUMBER

0 50

COUNTRY
FLAG

START BARS

QUIET ZONE

BEARER
BARS

FORM-LTD012 - I

SYMBOLOGY

EAN BAR CODE BREAKDOWN

CORNER MARKS

QUIET
ZONE

QUIET
ZONE

LIGHT
MARGIN
INDICATOR

LEFT
GUARD BAR

CENTRE
GUARD BAR

RIGHT
GUARD BAR

COUNTRY
FLAG

MANUFACTURER
NUMBER

PRODUCT
NUMBER

CHECK
DIGIT

HUMAN READABLES IN OCR B FONT

© COPYRIGHT SYMBOLOGY LTD 1991

FORM – LTD 011 – 1

A bar code symbol is a pattern of light and dark bars, or bars and spaces which encode a unique identity number. It can be read automatically by a laser scanner, just like a car number plate. The scanner projects a beam across the symbol. It monitors the reflected light and non-reflected light—black and white bars. The signals of reflected/non-reflected light are decoded into the identity number and, therefore, contrast is important. As the size of the bar code shrinks, the inaccuracy increases. Also, the scanner does not see the range of colours that the human eye does. Some colours are indistinguishable to it like gold and silver. So, it is important to have strong contrasts like black and yellow, or dark blue and red, or dark green and orange. The bar code must also be clearly printed on a flat surface of the unit.

It is possible to bar code price-off or other coupons. This, in fact, is done in the West to be able to electronically monitor redemptions and analyse promotions.

In India, bar coding has so far been used more commonly for inventory management by companies and internal control than for retail check-out counters, except in the few but growing number of supermarkets and malls. It is used relatively more in the garment trade and for export consignments and not so much in the independent million plus retail outlets because of the investments required in scanning technology. It is an interesting fact that in some cases, what look like bar codes are actually placed only to make the pack look more modern and are not really useable bar codes!

If you want to obtain bar codes for your brand and products you can get in touch with the Bar Code Association of India (www.eanindia.com). They will advise you of the formalities and the procedures, as well as allocate the bar code numbers to you.

Bar coding of products is virtually mandatory in the West and will soon be in Indian supermarkets and modern retail outlets. If your products do not already have bar codes, the sooner you obtain them, the better.

Bar coding and scanning make it easy to collect, store and analyse information, resulting not only in better inventory management but also in making detailed purchasing data a marketing tool for consumer-specific offers.

For example, in 1995, UK's largest retailer Tesco started a loyalty card, where consumers earn points on the basis of their spends. The points are stored on the card along with the purchase pattern of a particular consumer with Tesco. Not only does this promotion allow Tesco to try and win greater customer loyalty (the points can be redeemed for goods at the store) but also allows Tesco to:

+ Target specific promotions. For example, all Nescafe users are sent a direct mail about Tesco's premium coffee (which is perhaps 15 per cent cheaper), with an offer of a 50g creamer jar free.
+ Analyse which of these promotions are more successful.
+ Analyse what times of the day the purchasing is the greatest.
+ Gain insights into cross brand usage. For example, whether premium soap users are also premium shampoo users (which brands) and what are their toilet paper preferences. Do Diet Pepsi users also prefer decaffeinated products and, therefore, are

they potential customers for other low calorie and specialist products?

In the Customer's Own Words

Service industries like airlines are increasingly asking customers to provide them information regarding their preferences so that they can meet them. For example, an airline asks Mrs Gandhi, a 'frequent flyer club member', whether she prefers a vegetarian or non-vegetarian meal, an aisle seat or a window seat and then every time Mrs Gandhi books a ticket, this is done automatically for her. Think of her feelings when the booking agent tells her, 'and you would like a vegetarian meal and window seat as usual Ma'am wouldn't you?'

This is also typically done at the time of enrolling a member for a free service. Two examples are the enrollment forms for the free email service from rediffmail.com and indiatimes.com. Not only is the consumer's name and address collected, so is information pertaining to his/her interests and hobbies.

Obtaining Customer Feedback

Customer feedback can be obtained in various ways:

With Every Purchase or Delivery

- ◆ Hotels and restaurants are prime examples of this, with 'we'd like to hear from you' cards signed by the general manager placed in each room/table.

Via Mailed Questionnaire

- ◆ The key here is to keep the questionnaire as short and simple as possible.
- ◆ RCI (the holiday exchange company) regularly sends out a questionnaire to holiday makers after their trip.

By Telephone Research

- ◆ Check customer satisfaction on the phone. The key is to keep questions simple as possible. Minimize if not eliminate open-ended questions.
- ◆ Car companies do a lot of this sort of research.

Via a Third Party

- ◆ A market research firm, for example.
- ◆ This is done across firms and industries. Some well-known firms are: Gallurp and IMRB.

In Person (Face-to-Face)

- ◆ The best feedback to get is always active, direct and emotional face-to-face. You can't beat hearing what your customers think about you directly, seeing the look in their eyes, hearing the tone in their voice and watching their body language as they talk to you.
- ◆ This is the reason why in the best companies, managers necessarily make 'market visits' and observe or talk to consumers in the store/showroom, often completely unannounced. Every year, Hindustan Lever managers travel the length and

breadth of the company talking to stockists, retailers and consumers. Under a consumer contact programme, they even visit her kitchen to see the consumer cook and see her use a washing machine. Consumer familiarity breeds success!

Becoming a Mystery Consumer of Your Own Business

- Like the emperor in the story tale who wandered about anonymously amongst his subjects, try being an anonymous (or mystery) consumer of your own business. You will be amazed at what you will learn and you should not be afraid to find out!
- The key is to do this exercise anonymously.

Database Marketing

Obtaining detailed information on consumers can, as its logical conclusion, enable us to undertake one-to-one marketing. This involves database marketing.

Benefits of Database Marketing

Database marketing has grown in popularity and is expected to do so because of the better qualitative impact it has compared to mass media. Its benefits include:

- higher response;
- greater conversion;
- ability to cross sell, for example, saving bank accounts to credit card customers;

- opportunity to upsell, for example, Gold credit cards to Classic credit card customers;
- increased customer loyalty and retention due to personalization;
- targeted marketing and better segmentation;
- measurable performance;
- support for integrated marketing.

Setting Up a Marketing Database

Many companies already hold a database in some form such as:

- purchase records;
- enquiries and orders;
- account details;
- service records are kept on separate databases but it can and should be used;
- database can also be bought from database vendors on an outright or rental (usage only) basis;
- getting a good database is easier said than done.

Exercise: What are the sources of databases in your company?

Database Integrity and Accuracy

Data accuracy and integrity is critical. Imagine you proudly serve a non-vegetarian meal as the preferred choice to a stout Jain vegetarian! No marketing by your competitor could do a better job for them. For accuracy, a database needs to be:

- Cleaned : Deduced and sorted for address accuracy, etc.

- Enhanced : Adding the number of employees or turnover or industry type (to just name and address), for example.
- Profiled : Segregating the data into different groups.
- Updated : This needs to be done regularly because people and businesses change addresses. It would be best if you can devise a system that encourages 'data records' to themselves advise changes. For example, winning coupons will only be sent to the recorded addresses of the loyalty programme members.

All these activities are often undertaken with the help of specialist database agencies and consultants. The database is typically stored using software programmes like Access, SQL Server, or Oracle Legacy databases in Dbase and Foxpro can easily be upgraded to the new generation RDBMS packages. The advantage of using these relational databases is that many relationships can be established without compromising on database integrity.

Exercise: What would you need to do with the databases available in your company to make them useable?

Using the Database to Competitive Advantage

Once you have an accurate database, you can utilize it for competitive advantage and to practice CRM in your organization.

Building and Maintaining Top of Mind (TOM)

If Glaxo has a database of the leading doctors in India, it can regularly mail them a newsletter on the latest developments in the medical world. Glaxo could also invite articles and perhaps even pay for articles published in the magazine.

In order to be able to get the magazine, the doctors would need to keep their record with Glaxo updated. Finedge India did this successfully for Dabur by writing to Ayurvedic doctor offering a six-month free Ayurvedic magazine if they kept their details with us upgraded. A validated database of 33,000 *vaids* was created with whom we could and did have a regular communication.

Increasing Usage

If Hindustan Lever has a database of its tomato puree users, it can try and increase consumption by mailing them recipe booklets using tomato puree. Similarly, Bacardi can mail rum-based cocktail recipes to its users and create a romance around the product by narrating stories about who invented the cocktail and when.

Increasing Retention

Credit card companies telephone lapsed users and try and persuade them to retain their cards. The success rate can be 30 per cent plus, depending upon the skill of the telemarketer and how well he/she can overcome the problem for which the card was cancelled in the first place.

Airlines also use loyalty programmes which are run on the basis of points or miles earned, on the basis of the number of flights taken. These can then be redeemed for free flights or other freebies. A detailed account is kept of these miles and each frequent flyer is kept informed regularly about the points status. It is interesting to note that there is usually a point count (which gets depleted on taking free flights or room nights at hotels) and a category status like Gold, Silver or Blue, which is earned on the basis of the number of flights and miles but which wins service like guaranteed reservation and access to business-class lounges, even if you are travelling economy, and even if there are no miles left in the account.

Cross Sales

If Godrej Pillsbury has a database of consumers of its cooker cake mix, it can get a focused target market when it launches an eggless cake mix, and then a chocolate mix and so on. The database can help it try to achieve a greater share of the consumers' wallet.

Similarly, a bank can try and market all its products to a customer of any one of them, and thereby try and gain a 'greater share of the wallet'.

Improving Collections

Credit card companies and cellular phone companies amongst others use database telemarketing to help debt recoveries. Knowing the prospect's residence and office telephone numbers, and regularly calling on them is an effective way to this in many cases. In fact, if you don't have the right name and address, how do you collect payments?

Promoting Sales

Databases can also be used for directly or indirectly promoting sales. For example, an offer of a free test drive of the Fiat Sienna can be made to all Maruti owners and a small 'reward' can even be given for taking the test drive. This can be done by telemarketing or by direct mail.

Direct selling with the help of databases is also undertaken. For telemarketing, this is typically the case with high-value items like air conditioners and cards, while with direct mail it can be couponing for low unit value consumer goods too.

Churn Management

Database analysis can help in identifying potential consumers who may be in danger of becoming lapsed users, and thereby facilitate churn management. Sophisticated software exists which can predict this.

Customer Delight

Database marketing can also enable the achievement of that milestone beyond satisfaction—customer delight.

Imagine what you would feel about an international airline which told you when you were checking in that 'this is your 25th flight with us, sir. We would like to upgrade you to a first class seat', or what your reaction would be if you were told that 'you bought a fridge from us five years ago and are now buying a TV. We would like to give you a certificate which you or any of your friends can exchange for a 15 per cent discount of an LG product'. This is recognition for being a loyal user. What is the consumer's likely choice when he next buys a consumer durable and what would be the word of mouth value of that 15 per cent discount certificate?

Exercise:

- ○ For what purpose is your database best used?
- ○ What would be more useful for you—direct mail, or telemarketing, or both?
- ○ How would you commence database marketing if your company did not have a database?

Points to Remember

- The better you know your customer, the better you can serve him. So, try and get as much information about him/her as practicable.
- Valuable databases often exist within the company—so look before buying from outside.
- Database integrity and accuracy are critical for the success of the programme.
- Databases can be used for competitive advantage at various stages of the marketing cycle and for practising CRM. Decide the objectives and then plan the activity.
- Database marketing has a higher qualitative impact than mass mailing.

Chapter 4

CRM in Call Centres

O NE of the most useful ways CRM is practised is through call centres or customer contact centres that are specifically set up to handle customer interactions. These are often by telephone (sometimes toll free) but can equally be by email or traditional mail, or a combination of all three, and are referred to as 'helplines' or 'carelines'.

Carelines are set up to basically cater to existing consumers. There is a growing realization that retaining old customers is easier and far more profitable than getting new ones.

Careline Objectives

One of the objectives of a careline is to facilitate complaints by consumers. Why should one do that? A Nielsen study done in western Europe in the early 1990s showed that only one in 50 consumers complain. The other 49 simply change brands. So, the idea is to facilitate complaints and resolve them because research also shows that a consumer who complains and is then satisfied has a more positive attitude towards the brand than one who had no complaint at all!

Exercise: What did you do when you last had a problem with a product? What would you have done had there been a careline number readily available?

Toll Free

In an increasingly competitive world, it is important to make it easier for people to buy your products and to get help or answers to questions or problems than your competitors do. As a gesture indicating that it is a company's privilege to have a consumer call, carelines are often toll free which means it is the company and not the calling customer who pays for the call. In the US, toll free or 1–800 numbers are seen as a right, not a privilege, and virtually all goods and services have this facility.

A toll-free service called Freephone by MTNL was launched in India in November 1998. As of January 2005, it is presently available in a network of 171 cities. More cities will be added in a phased manner. Freephone is like a normal phone call except that the caller has to dial a 10-digit number starting 1600. Only MTNL and BSNL currently offer Freephone services though a similar service from other landlines and cellular service providers is imminent. A Freephone number cannot currently be accessed from a cellular phone. When a call is made to a

Freephone there is no charge to the caller—the called party pays. In the West, this is typically a flat rate which is quite low. In India, however, so far, MTNL charges base the STD charges between the calling and called city but gives a 30 per cent discount on the rate.

Exercise: How many of the customers of your company actually write or call? How long does it take for the company to respond? What would you like the ideal situation to be?

Not Just for Complaints

Ideally, a careline should be set up not only to handle complaints but also to provide assistance in using the product. For example, the Reckitt Healthy Home Careline (1–600–11–2233) handles not only complaints on Mortein, Lizol and Dettol but also gives tips to consumers on how to keep their home healthy. Pillsbury Cooker Cake Mix 'Namaste Pillsbury' Careline (1–600–111–789) not only helps consumers with problems relating to the product but also provides recipes for icing and solicits new product ideas.

The Dominos helpline (1–600–111–123) directs consumers to the outlets nearest to them, making it easy for customers to order their pizzas. Note the easy to remember number.

A careline can also help support brand positioning and can be the differentiator between brands. For example, Asian Paints has set up a helpline (1–901–333–355) where consumers can get free assistance in the choice of colour, price comparisons, etc. This free advice enables them to be seen as a friendly and helpful paint expert.

Godrej Response Centre
1-600-225511

Refrigerators
Washing Machines
SmartCare Appliance Service
Locks
Home Furniture
Office Furniture
Security Equipment

We're just a call away.

For Whirlpool Consumer Service

please call

51666333

We listen, We care. We're always there.

Exercise:

- ○ Which other helplines can you think of? Call them and ask different questions. .
- ○ Assuming you had a product complaint, check a pack of Kissan Annapurna Atta and Cargill's Nature Fresh Atta. What would you do in each case?
- ○ Which of your products would you like to have a careline? What additional consumer benefit could you propose?

A Careline is Useful for Market Research

A careline provides a useful early warning system for complaints. The company has the name and telephone number of the complainant and so can research her at length. Calls can also be made later to find out usage habits and patterns of not only that product but related and competitive products.

The consumer who calls the careline is quite involved with the product—or else she would not make the effort. Hence, she is an excellent respondent to provide insights. Having a list of such respondents facilitates a quick usage and attitude study or other types of research. A listing exercise is not necessary and the research can be done in days rather than weeks.

Exercise: Ask for a quotation for a short usage and attitude study from a call centre and a traditional market research firm. Compare the costs and time taken for the study.

A Careline Helps Launch Brand Extensions

A careline helps build a database and can be used for database marketing and brand extensions. For example, Pillsbury has a database of pressure cooker cake mix users. It can research these or coupon them when it is launching a strawberry cake mix.

How Does a Careline Operate?

Although email is becoming increasingly popular, the telephone is still the most popular medium for carelines. This is because compared to a letter it is fast, direct and gives an immediate response. The telephone is also more reliable in terms of uptime and language, accent compatibility and understanding of the caller and the Customer Service Representative (CSR).

This language/accent problem does not exist for email and more carelines in future could be based on web chats, as the email gains in popularity.

Exercise:
- Compare your willingness to write a letter to complain vis-à-vis if you had to make a telephone call/send an email.
- Find out the number of telephone and Internet connections in India and the rate at which they are expected to grow.

Setting Up and Managing a Careline

Some of the issues that require careful thought while setting up and managing a careline are given in the following pages.

Outsourced or In-house?

Many companies prefer to outsource this important activity to specialized call centres. Others regard the data as too important and confidential to be given outside the company and run the call centre in-house. For example, Godrej Appliances has an in-house call centre, whereas Whirlpool has outsourced it.

Centralized or Decentralized?

Typically, across the world, a company's call centre is centralized to have better quality and control. However, because of relatively high telecom costs (India's rates are amongst the highest in the world) some have chosen to have more than one. For example, ICICI Bank and Tata AIG Insurance have one centralized call centre, whereas Asian Paints and Whirlpool have more than one call centre in India.

Capital Intensity

The industry is fairly capital intensive with investments required not only in real estate but in computer and telephone hardware and software and in networking.

Technological Obsolescence

This is a new field with new products—both hardware and software being regularly launched. Clearly, an area of 'creative destruction' like the rest of the IT industry, and so a choice has to be made 'when to cut in'.

Retention of Staff

Critical to the successful handling of a call is the skill, training and motivation of the CSR. Yet, the typical 'shelf life' of CSRs are six months to a year, as they find the job repetitive and boring. This phenomena is common the world over. In India, this is accentuated by the fact that the number of call centres is mushrooming and so there is a shortage of trained CSRs.

Training

Adequate training is critical to success. This involves training in:

- ◆ communication;
- ◆ telephone manners;
- ◆ product knowledge;
- ◆ infrastructure knowledge—telephony and software.

Predicting the Call Volume

The entire careline operation is more or less modular. But expensive telephones, computer and software have to be bought on the basis of forecast of call volumes. In the absence of previous experience, this is a difficult task.

Exercise: If Hindustan Lever set up a helpline for Surf, how many calls would there be daily if the number was toll free (*a*) on the pack; and (*b*) also on TV?

Monitoring Performance

Performance is monitored quantitatively by the reports of the Automatic Call Distributor (ACD)—what percentage of calls were picked up after more than two rings, the average call waiting time, the maximum waiting time, etc. It is also monitored qualitatively by supervisors listening in (anonymously) to CSRs talking, and by listening to tape-recorded conversations later.

Exercise:

- Visit a call centre with an ACD and ask to see the supervisor's phone.
- Try to listen in to a conversation.
- Call the Resort Condominium International (RCI) helpline (080–5587898) for booking a resort.

Cost-benefit Analysis

The costs of a call centre are easy to calculate. The benefits may not be so easy to quantify. However, the real value needs to be established—life-time value of retained customers, advertisement value of delighted customers, positive word of mouth generated and the market intelligence and insight gained.

Exercise: List all the benefits of your careline and quantify each. Then do a cost-benefit analysis (if your company does not have a careline, try and guestimate the numbers).

Service and Checking it Out

Check out how your company's service yourself like the king who wandered the streets like an ordinary person to know what was really going on. When going on a market visit or visit to your product dealers, ask to see the market or dealer other than the one in your tour programme. Choose to visit some customers at random.

Telephone Conversations

It is easy to check this—you need to just record the conversations. One gets special tape-recorders at barely Rs 1,500 each that automatically go on and off when the phone is being used. Use them for quality checks and training. Some issues that you may notice are:

- Voices need to reflect the confidence of the speaker.
- You need to identify yourself in a call to make it personal.
- You need to be careful while keeping customers on hold. Customers may be able to hear all that is being said.
- Objection handling needs to be structured. Standard responses to common objections needs to be scripted and used by everybody.
- Listening is a gap. People are either distracted or not giving the customer their full attention. The result is needless repetition and lengthening of call.
- Over the phone, words if not spoken clearly and at a steady pace, sound like they are running together.

- It is important to probe and get the customer to speak as much as possible.
- We do not sell, the customer buys. So, allow the customer time and thinking space to buy if you are wanting to sell.

We have appended two simple quality assessment sheets below—one for inbound service calls, and one for outbound sales calls. You will notice the emphasis on 'probing' is greater in the selling call because we want to engage the customer and uncover his needs.

QUALITY AUDIT SHEET (INBOUND)		
CSR Name:		
Process:		
Date of Monitoring:		
Auditor's Name:		
	Call 1	Score
Opening Bracket		
Call Opening		
Authentication of Customer Information		
Asked His Name and Other Relevant Information		
Listening Bracket		
Does not Interrupt the Customer		
Exhibits Responsiveness Towards Customers		
Does not Make Assumptions		
Speaking Bracket		
Appropriate Usage of Customer Name		

(*Contd.*)

Clarity in Speech		
Courtesy and Politeness		
Rate of Speech		
Appropriate Usage of Hold Script		
Empathy Towards Customer		
Usage of Appropriate Grammar		
Tone Used on the Call		
Avoid Usage of Jargon, Acronyms, Slang		
Troubleshooting Bracket		
Paraphrased the Customer Issue		
Relevant Probing Being Done		
Complete and Correct Information Provided		
Alternatives Suggested		
System Skills/Resource Usage Bracket		
Used Available Resources Well		
Complete and Accurate Customer Information		
Closing Bracket		
Trial Closing		
Additional Needs Uncovered		
Correct Closing		

Overall Score on the Call

Summary of the Call

(*Contd.*)

(Contd.)

Areas of Improvement (Feedback for the Areas of Improvement for the CSR)

What Went Well (Feedback for the Things CSR did Well on the Call)

QUALITY AUDIT SHEET (OUTBOUND)			
Name of Team Member			
Department			
Date			
Auditor's Name	Call		
Parameter	**Score**	**Y/N**	**Comments**
Opening			
Good Morning/Afternoon/ Evening			
Introducing Yourself by Name			
Mention Organization Name			
Check the Availability			
Asking for Time Availability from the Customer to Speak for Few Minutes			

(Contd.)

Objective of the Call			
Explaining the Customer About the Objective of the Call			
Probe			
Questions in Symmetry with the Process			
Product Knowledge			
Complete Knowledge About the Product and Services			
Able to Explain All Product Details			
Ready with All Types of FAQS			
Explained Clearly the Procedure to Get the Services			
Told As to How it is Beneficial			
Listening Skills			
Paraphrasing			
Exhibits Responsiveness Towards Customers			
Listens to All Queries Without Interruption			
Tone			
Warm and Friendly/Blunt/ Harsh or Aggressive			If tone has all the 3 parameters OK

(*Contd.*)

Enthusiastic/Unenthusiastic Concerned/Customer Oriented/Casual			then=3 or else depending upon the no. of parameters found in the tone give relevant marks
Expressive/Non-expressive Modulation in the Tone/ No Modulation Intonation Followed/ No Intonation			If tone has all the 3 parameters OK then=3 or else depending upon the no. of parameters found in the tone give relevant marks
Speech			
Flow Fluent/Broken			
Audible Loud/Soft-spoken			
Communication			
Clarity			
Pace and Modulation			
Pronunciation of Words and Phrases			
Distinctive Without Any Blank Air			
Customer Service			
Usage of Valuing Statements			
Quality Time Spent to Understand Customers Need			

(*Contd.*)

Personalizing the Call			
Closing Wraping of Call			
Check Understanding/ Satisfaction			
Offering Further Assistance			
Mentioning Your and Organization's Name			
Thanked the Customer for their Time			
Allows Customer to Hang Up First			
Total QA Score			
1-Unacceptable; 2-Satisfactory; 3-Good Total Score Out of 90 Score>=81 Good Score<81 & S>= 68 Satisfactory Score<68 & S>54 Unacceptable Score<54 Critical Concern			Agent's signature

Points to Remember

- Lapsed users can be reduced by making it easy for consumers with complaints to contact the company, like through a careline.
- A careline can be by phone, email or traditional mail, or a combination of these.

- The careline is a consumer contact centre and can be used for establishing positioning, achieving consumer delight, market research.
- A call centre is a state of the art facility requiring considerable investment in computer and telephone hardware and software.
- CSRs are the voice of the company to the consumer. Their skills, knowledge and motivation are critical. But typically, their 'shelf life' the world over tends to be short.
- The success of the call centre depends upon various choices a company makes depending upon its circumstances. But adequate planning and thought of the various issues must be made.
- In an evaluation of a call centre, the life-time value of retained customers and other qualitative factors must be considered as part of the cost-benefit analysis.

Chapter 5

CRM One-to-One

CRM can be impersonal through mass media, personalized through direct marketing (mail, email or telephonic), or personal through face-to-face contact.

Personal selling is of the last type and is pervasive in B2B selling, industrial sales and sales of services.

Selling is a form of communication where the objective is to get a desired response through a stimuli.

But before understanding selling, let us understand how communication works. Communication comes from the Latin *communis* which means to 'establish commonness'. By communication we try and establish a commonness with the targeted recipient of our communication. The message emanates in the mind, is encoded into a message and sent through a medium (can be face-to-face, phone, fax, email, SMS) to the recipient to be decoded. The message can only be decoded if it is received. So, it is essential that the recipient has the same medium as the sender. For example, if an SMS message is sent and the recipient's mobile is not working, it will not reach and the communication will be incomplete. Similarly, if a fax is sent and there is no paper at the other end, the whole point of the communication is lost.

Assuming the message is received, communication will depend upon the language being understood by both. For example, if someone speaks in English to another who understands only Hindi, there will be no communication! Similarly, if a person nods his head to mean 'yes' whereas the other understands it to mean 'no', there will be miscommunication because instead of 'yes', 'no' will be understood!

So, it is critical that the sender and receiver speak the same language, and the greater the common field of experience and knowledge, the better the communication will be. That is why communication is so good and misunderstanding is rare between close friends. Viewed conceptually:

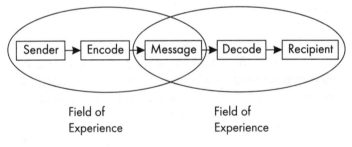

Field of
Experience

Field of
Experience

The greater one's field of experience, the better one is likely to communicate, whether face-to-face, phone, email, fax or SMS. Also the greater the commonness in the field of experience between sender and receiver, the better will be the communication. Which is why communication is easier and better between people from the same communities, and those who travel more and have greater life experiences can communicate better.

Some Points to Ponder

- ❑ Who do you find it easiest to communicate with?
- ❑ Who do you think you would find it most difficult to communicate with?
- ❑ What does the speed of communication depend upon?
- ❑ What does clarity of communication and lack of misunderstanding depend upon?

Now let us look at face-to-face communication. Research indicates that even in this kind of communication, only 7 per cent of the communication is the words used; 55 per cent of new face-to-face communication is non-verbal body language, i.e., how we sit, how we look, how we are dressed and what we do with our hands while talking. The balance 38 per cent is voice quality. Yes, even in face-to-face communication, voice quality is 38 per cent versus 7 per cent for words used!

In one-to-one CRM, or should one say communication management or persuasion, every interaction matters and one needs to look at an integrated approach as defined in chapter 1 for product services marketing. After all, personal selling or CRM one-to-one is nothing but marketing oneself.

So, in terms of the 8P model (in chapter 2) what does one need to do to be successful 'one-to-one'?

Product/Packaging

Be well groomed and smartly attired. Bankers wear suits to present a serious image of themselves. B2B selling is serious business. One needs to look the part—neat hair cut, clean and cut nails, well-kept beard or clean shaven as the case may be. One must also be 'suitably' attired. For example, a sari or *salwar* suit may be a more appropriate dress than a business suit for a lady going to meet a traditional Marwari businessman. After all, the objective is to establish 'commonness', not intimidate or awe!

In one-to-one selling you are 'selling yourself' besides the product you are selling. So, you need to be knowledgeable about the buyers' needs, his business and the details of your product/service and competition. You are part of the 'offering' to the consumer!

Personality

The sales representative is part of the brand personality. If there is little or no mass media as in the case of many industrial products or international marketing, he is the brand/product personality. It is essential to be personable, ideal to be likeable. After all, the probability of an order is greater if the buyer likes the sales person than if he doesn't. We act not only by how we think but also how we feel.

Price

Here the concept is what Kotler calls 'the transaction cost'. What is the transaction cost in doing the deal with the sales person of company X. Is he always on time, well-groomed, and well-informed, courteous and makes the buyer 'feel good' about himself and the decision to buy? Chances are that he will get the order over a seller who may even have a slightly better offering objectively but argues with the buyer, doesn't show up on time, makes false promises and is not well-informed.

Passion

In one-to-one interaction, passion or love of one's product and company is noticeable and often the differentiator between success and failure. All great sales people are passionate about their wares. They believe them to be the best and this feeling tends to rub off. After all, if you are not passionate about your product, how can you expect someone else to be?

Promotion

In order to establish a greater rapport, it is helpful if there is a shared common interest. Hospitality is an example of building better communication and persuasion—business lunches, taking buyers to see cricket matches, conferences in exotic places, festival gifts and greetings. See how you can build a personal relationship with existing or potential buyers. Some of the more popular ways are— find out if they play golf or bridge or tennis and invite them to play with you (provided you play!), preferably at some exclusive club. Alternatively, invite the prospect to an exciting restaurant or pubs or to a play, depending upon his interest.

Another way of building a relationship is to remember birthdays, anniversaries and festivals and send gifts/ greetings. But care needs to be taken that the latter are appropriate depending upon the relationship.

Promoting a relationship one-to-one should be done carefully and intelligently.

People

Apart from the direct company sales person, successful one-to-one relationships depend upon the rest of the team—your receptionist, your secretary, your after-sales service team, your customer care department. The one-to-one relationship is impacted by all other points of interaction with the company. This needs to be understood not only by the company sales person but by the rest of the team as well. How they communicate—content and style—will impact the one-to-one relationship and so CRM needs to pervade the organization if the one-to-one relationship is to be positively affected.

Place

How easily and readily is the sales person available and how quickly he responds, naturally affects the one-to-one relationship. It helps if the sales person meets the buyer's deadline to quote even if it is very short. If he is on call at 9 pm (if necessary) without a problem. If he keeps his appointments and regularly calls on the prospects. Just keeping in touch and developing a relationship even when there is no immediate work in hand, helps in relationship and business development. To use a Coke analogy, the sales person should be 'at arms length of (the buyer's) desire' to contact.

Positioning

In order to develop long-term success, there is no alternative but for the seller to develop a positioning in the buyers mind as reliable, honest and above all trustworthy. If the buyer does not see the sales person as trustworthy, how will he willingly agree to deal with him and his company. The sales person is the face of the company's brand and must inspire trust, or else there will be problems and an unhealthy one-to-one relationship. This means that the sales person must do nothing that could destroy his personal credibility. He must guard his reputation at all cost and position himself as a trustworthy and reliable business associate who believes in a win-win situation and is always concerned with long-term mutual benefits.

In order to know how you and your company are in reality performing, it is useful to do a customer satisfaction survey once a year. The questionnaire we use is given below:

Customer Satisfaction Survey

1. Which five words/phrases best describe XYZ Co. as you see it?
   (i)
   (ii)
   (iii)
   (iv)
   (v)
2. In what areas do you like XYZ Co. working the most?
3. In what areas would you like XYZ Co. to be better at?
4. How satisfied are you with XYZ Co. overall?
   A. Would recommend to others ☐
   B. Satisfied ☐
   C. Not quite satisfied ☐
   D. Very dissatisfied ☐
5. What new opportunities are there in the foreseeable future of working together?
6. Any suggestions of any kind.

In fact, if you go to the logical extension of the concept and treat all your constituents as your customers—your direct subordinates, your peers, your boss and your family, you can adapt the customer satisfaction survey form as follows:

360 Degree Feedback
Appraised: *Appraisee:*   *Appraisal Period:*   Months
Appraisee Relationship with Appraised: Note: Please be frank in your response.

1. What five words/phrases best describe the appraised?
    (i)
    (ii)
    (iii)
    (iv)
    (v)
 2. What do you think are the appraised four biggest strengths?
    (i)
    (ii)
    (iii)
    (iv)
 3. What areas would you like the concerned to be better at?
    (i)
    (ii)
    (iii)
    (iv)
 4. How do you think your relationship with the concerned can be improved?
    (i)
    (ii)
    (iii)
    (iv)

Use this form across your constituents and you will have a 360-degree feedback about yourself. It will be you as others see you. And that is the important part—whether you are considering the situation as the company or yourself. What is the perception (which is often more important than reality)? What do you want to change?

How can you change it? By when will you change it? That is how you can use your customers own words to help you serve them better. One-to-one. One by one.

Points to Remember

- The principles of one-to-one CRM are no different than plain vanilla CRM. One-to-one CRM is personal whereas CRM is personalized. To that extent, one-to-one marketing is the ultimate form of CRM.
- The one-to-one relationship must be managed by both what a buyer thinks and what he feels.
- The sales person is part of the brand offering and, in fact, especially of industrialized products. He is the face of the brand.
- The one-to-one relationship is impacted not only by the direct one-to-one contact but also by the buyer's interactions with other support departments in the seller's company. So, it is important for the total experience to be good.
- A critical factor in the one-to-one relationship is the personal qualities of the sales person. He must be able to inspire trust and confidence and the buyer should like/enjoy dealing with them.

Chapter 6

The Sound of Service

IN the context of CRM, whenever the thought of talking to someone for service comes up, the image that is conjured up is of hundreds of people, with headphones on, sitting in front of computer screens in giant call centres. Impersonal, detached—anything but conducive to relationship building!

The essence of CRM is getting to know the customer better, and that means greater personal interaction, with individual attention. The customer interacts with a representative of the company, his information is captured in a database, tabulated, analysed and used to customize the product to his needs. It may be a tangible product, it may be an intangible service and it may even be an intangible service for a very tangible product. The emphasis here, is on individual interaction. The customer talks to a human representative of the corporation. A human, with all his imperfections. The impact of the interaction is, therefore, dependent completely on this humble individual, who, most of the time, does not even realize his importance in the customer life-cycle.

The customer life-cycle is a concept akin to the product life-cycle from a different perspective. When we buy a product, we get into a relationship with the company that made the product. Whether our relationship will be a happy one or not, depends on:

+ whether the product meets our needs;
+ whether the product is of a quality that we expect;
+ the type of things that go wrong with the product; and
+ how the company treats us when something goes wrong with the product.

The first three points are completely controllable by mechanics—product design, input quality, production values and quality control. The last one brings us back to the human being at one end of the service chain.

Nature of Communication

Communication about a product can, therefore, be in one way—the advertising, the packaging, the promotions associated with the brand, or, it can be in two ways—at the sales point and at the service point. Increasingly, with more and more self-service retails outlets, the customer does not even meet the sales person at the sales point. On the other hand, telemarketing has gained favour, and the one-on-one interaction finds its outlet here.

The focus needs to be on why customers talk to representatives of the company they have just bought a product from:

- when the company contacts the customer to ask them if they want the product or service they are offering;
- when they want a product or service and contact the company or company representative for it;
- when they know about the product but want more information about it; or
- when something goes wrong and the customer calls the company to fix it.

Apart from the first point above, the customer initiates the contact with the company. This is a very powerful situation. Here is a customer, who feels involved enough with the product to take the initiative to contact the company.

What do we do with this tentative feeler for starting a relationship? How does the company representative respond? Does he or she respond in a manner that would further the relationship and cement the image of the product in the customers' mind?

Appropriateness of Response

So far, all the customer has received, is one-way communication. A golden opportunity has arisen for the company to listen to the customer and respond. The appropriateness of the response is the essence of the need to address the issue of 'The Sound of Service' in this chapter. Too often, the company representative—the receptionist at the sales office, the customer service agent in the call centre, or the service engineer arriving at the customer's home—have no idea of how to respond appropriately.

Appropriateness does not just mean 'politeness' in this context. It means, appropriate in the context of the image of the brand. If the brand is a bank, what should the response sound like? If the brand is a luxury hotel, what should the response sound like? Would you as a customer expect the same quality of response from ICICI Bank, as you would from The Oberoi Hotel? To take the argument further, *should* ICICI Bank sound like The Oberoi, or vice versa?

The choice of what this response should be and the implementation of a game plan to ensure that each customer touch point responds in the *appropriate* way to the customer, is objective of creating a strategy to create 'The Sound of Service'.

The Sound of Service Strategy

Create the 'Sound of Service'

In earlier chapters, the 'Band' strategy for brands was referred to. Brands are nothing but images in our mind. These images are formed by a combination of the messages we get about a brand from various media. These could be promotions (advertising and sales promotions), packaging, pricing and, of course, the product itself. The image is reinforced constantly by following the 'Band' strategy. These are all forms of the one-way communication and is part of a smoothly rolled out campaign.

As markets become fragmented and companies increasingly reach out to the individual customer, the reason why CRM is such a burning issue in the current day becomes clear. The customer is also more discerning and demands quality and service. When it falls short, she does not hesitate to contact the company and demand her just due.

What should this interaction sound like, is a conscious decision a company must take. Should it be formal or informal? What language should it be in? Open-ended or structured? It is a reflection of how a company wants its customers to be treated. For example, at The Oberoi, no matter who you ask for help, the problem is seamlessly resolved. At ICICI Bank, the problem resolution could take 24 hours. This is not to say that The Oberoi way is better. The point is to highlight that both are different and consciously so.

It is not possible to demand the 'Oberoi' standard of service just because it is the best. This quality comes at a price that customers may not be willing to pay. The low-cost airline revolution is the pinnacle of this strategy. They do not provide in-flight service and are proud of the fact. They are also very successful. When they are called to cancel a ticket, you are told by an Interactive Voice Response (IVR), not even a human voice, that you will need to visit the airport to do so. A conscious sound of service—they do not want to spend money on a CSR to do a job that the machine does so well. The customers too, do not expect it—it is all part of the 'Band' strategy.

The 'Sound of Service' is an exercise akin to making a vision statement. Think of it as a service vision and ensure that all customers, internal and external, hear the

company's voice, just as the company intended them to
hear it.

Identify Customer Touch Points

The number of people that need to be informed of what
their company's 'Sound of Service' should be, are all those
that come in contact with customers. The main customer
touch points are:

- the sales staff;
- the service staff;
- the call centre;
- the telephone operator at the company switch-
  board;
- the retailer who stocks the product;
- the distributor salesmen who distribute the product to the trade;
- the home-delivery man;
- the pick-up man;
- the outsourced agency conducting a direct marketing campaign;
- the service engineer;
- the finance department that handles vendor
  payments;
- the purchase department that negotiates with vendors;
- your colleagues!

In most organizations, the sales, service and call centre
staff receive all the attention, as they are the obvious char-
acters in the customer life-cycle drama. But what about
all the rest? As companies get leaner, the number of
outsourced operations increases. How do outsourced

vendors sound? For a customer, there is no distinction between a company employee and an outsourced vendor. For her, both of them are the face of the company. She will not understand why one is able to 'sound' right and the other does not.

A sense of uniformity in the way all transactions related to a product are handled, lends a dependability to the product that is hard to match. At each point, the customer knows what to expect and knows how she will be treated. It is when a jarring note is sounded by one off-key, is when things begin to unravel very quickly. It is at this point when statistics of the Technical Assistant Research Programs Inc. (TARP) survey of 1997 (www.tarp.com) appear starkly before one's eyes—a customer who experiences bad service, talks to 49 other people about it.

Breaking the 'Sound of Service' Down into its Components

We have been talking about an abstract idea of creating a sound of service. Specifically, this means the communication style a company must adopt. Communication has a verbal and a non-verbal aspect to it. In fact, it is the non-verbal part that often makes the greater impact, rather than the verbal part. Therefore, the sound of service is really a misnomer, as the non-verbal element is just as important as the verbal element.

Verbal and non-verbal communication is made up of many components. The components that make the most impact, have been listed below:

- choice of language;
- consonant sounds;

- vowel sounds;
- grammar;
- speech defects;
- pronunciation;
- fillers and foghorns;
- tone;
- pace;
- intonation;
- pausing and blending;
- listening;
- paraphrasing;
- empathy;
- building rapport;
- script;
- adherence to script;
- personalization;
- greeting;
- grooming;
- body language;
- eye contact.

It is possible to use each of these elements and decide against it, what the communication style of the company will be. For example, is it important for company representatives to speak in English or is it acceptable for them to speak in a regional language? At The Oberoi, the default language is English but should you speak in Hindi, you will find that you will be answered in Hindi. At the Maruti showroom, you may be taken around by a salesperson who does not know English but speaks excellent Hindi. Is it all right for him not to know English? This is a decision that a company must take consciously as it has an impact on the company's image. Again, is it essential to speak in a grammatically correct way? Sales people of Eureka Forbes, speak English but not correctly. Sales people at the Maurya, speak impeccable English. Both are extremely effective. Eureka Forbes realizes that correct grammar is not a critical requirement for their target audience, Maurya knows that poor grammar would reflect poorly on the hotel brand.

Each parameter listed above needs to be defined along with its acceptable level of performance. It is also important to assign weights to each of these parameters. If each parameters' performance level is defined, the HR department will be asked to go out and hire the 'ideal' profile. This is theoretically an excellent idea but practically, it is next to impossible to find candidates that fulfill all criteria. That is the importance of weights. Each company must decide which element of the sound of service is most important for it. It is useful to have three or maximum four parameters that comprise 80 per cent of the weightage. The number of parameters is easy to control and the ones that are not critical, can be trained.

Script design is an art that is hugely underestimated. The words that a company chooses to express itself are as clear an indicator of the company's self-image, as is an individual's language. The difference between saying 'Hi. May I help you?' over the phone and saying 'Good Evening. How may I help you today?'is stark. In fact, it formed the very basis of the Hutch campaign and brought to mind a fun, informal, friendly company. Did the rest of their sound of service follow suit? Call the Hutch call centre and find out!

It can be seen how huge an advantage, parameterizing the entire communication process of the company can be. All customer touch points now know what is expected of them. Even without being trained to sound a certain way, they can adapt their own communication styles to blend with what the company requires of them. The HR department knows clearly who it can hire and who it should not. Anyone who has problems that are not 'trainable' should not be taken on board, as they will never be able to gel with the company's service vision. Communicate the service vision to implement the sound of service strategy.

People are creatures of habit. Record a conversation you are having with a friend and then play it back. Try and identify the figures of speech that you use. Some are very common. Words such as 'Like', 'Basically', 'I mean', 'OK' are used so often, that we don't even focus on them any more. Try and also identify how your speech is different from your friends in the choice of words, the use of complete sentences, and the tendency to switch from one language to another. Now try and say the same thing without using any of your typical idioms or fillers. It is hard, isn't it?

You may feel that you are good worker and have always performed well. There is nothing wrong with the way you speak and, therefore, there is no reason to change it. Change of any kind is always resisted. Therefore, if the company wants to implement a sound of service strategy across the organization, it is going to face resistance in wondrous ways.

The important thing then, is to communication the need for change in a manner that anyone who is impacted by it appreciates 'Whats in it for me?' We are not only creatures of habit, we are selfish too! Unless we see something that benefits us, we don't see a need for making an effort to change anything whether it is the way we dress, our hair, the time we come to work, the work processes we follow, and so on.

Employees at customer touch points must be clearly shown the benefit of the sound of service strategy, where they will be asked to walk and talk in a certain way, using certain scripts and work processes. The challenge lies in relating this benefit to their individual job performance.

In a classic case we came across, CSRs in a bank were asked to greet all customers who came in with a smile. After putting them through a training programme, one month later, they were evaluated. It was found that no one was smiling and greeting the customer! When they were asked why they were not doing so, they said, 'What's in it for me (WIIFM)? Why should I smile? I am serving the customer to the best of my ability and if I smile, my performance evaluation does not get affected. All my manager wants is sales. He doesn't care how I greet them'. A clear case of not establishing the WIIFM.

To make people accept a new standard, requires a cultural shift. The hospitality industry and call centres in the West have understood this and their indoctrination begins as soon as a new employee enters the organization. Try and call directory enquiry in the UK. You will get the same tone and the same words every time. Try visiting a Thrifty Car Rental in Australia—they will greet you and ask you the same set of questions every time. They explain your liabilities and car features in exactly the same sequence, whichever outlet you go to. Consistency brings with it comfort—you know you are in the right place, and you know what to expect.

When new employees come into the organization, they must immediately be told about the service vision of the company and what is expected of them. This will go a long way in ensuring an openness to training, once the actual programme begins. What of existing employees? They have to be given the WIIFM too. A good way to do it is through videos, where employees are shown how they sound before and how they will sound after. A pilot run at a few customer touch points will bring out starkly the impact of using the sound of service in a real situation.

Any programme created to introduce employees to the sound of service strategy must be sensitive to the existing culture. The programme must be interactive and the facilitator must guide the session in a manner that elicits the desired outcome from the participants themselves. This way their buy-in is much stronger, rather than being issued a diktat on the new procedures.

Training

Once the organization has decided on a service vision and a communication style—jointly forming the sound of service strategy, the method through which this will be communicated to the ranks, needs to be chosen.

Just communicating the vision is not enough—people may choose to implement it in individual ways and the impact would be severely diluted. A structured programme needs to be created that will take into account the varied profiles of people in the organization, their roles and the nature of their interaction with the customer. For example, in a bank, the teller's role is highly repetitive and tightly structured. The way the teller needs to implement the sound of service strategy is very different from what a branch manager of the same bank would need to do. The branch manager's communication is highly unstructured, as she can be called in to handle any situation in the branch. The problems she faces would vary greatly in the degree of complexity. The training the branch manager will receive will, therefore, have a different focus.

The essence of the programme needs to remain the same. How the organization's employees will look, greet, respond or probe will be similar in a manner that is recognizable. To take the example of the bank further, if all employees are to speak in English, it will be relatively simple to teach the teller the frequently used phrases she will encounter. The branch manager on the other hand, will need a complete language course if she is not able to speak the language fluently. This is because it is not possible to predict the situation she is likely to face.

The point to be emphasized, is that even with a company-wide service vision and a unique communication style, the temptation to use a one-size-fits-all training programme should be avoided. Due to logistic complications and the financial impact of having different programmes for the different roles in the organization, this is a route most companies follow. The result—information overload for some levels and utter boredom for others. There are a few in the happy middle who enjoy the programme and actually take something away from it.

Training Content

The training programme could have many different elements in it, depending on what parameters the company has decided to adopt as part of its own sound of service strategy. Training could range from voice training, scripting, grooming, presentation skills, probing and so on. Think of the company that wanted to serve its customers better and put its CSRs through a customer service programme. When customer satisfaction levels were measured two weeks after the programme, there was no change at all. An analysis was done and it was found that since the CSRs were dealing with customers over email, what they needed was a training in email etiquette and writing, and not on customer service!

Assessments

The training programme must always be accompanied by assessments. Assessments must be at the individual level to ensure that each employee has understood what is required of him and is implementing it in the manner the company expects him to. Assessment design is a science that is highly under-rated and where the adage of 'garbage in garbage out' holds most aptly. The assessments must measure the very things that the company has decided are important in making an impact with their sound of service.

Assessment methodology has developed greatly over the past few years, and while assessment centres and simulations can result in extremely accurate results, it is not always possible, in time and money terms, to run these assessments.

Simple assessment techniques using role plays, in-box situations and rubrics can also be used effectively, provided the company and the service provider are clear about the end result.

Building Sustainability

We have traversed a long road by now. From designing a strategy to designing a programme to train employees to implement this strategy. But changing habits is hard. A 16 or 30 hour programme is unlikely to make a radical shift in people's behaviour. Most companies cannot spare more time than this on a single intervention. How then can we ensure that once introduced, the strategy is sustained. Over time, as new entrants come into the organization, a culture will spread and it will become easier but in the short term, close supervision and monitoring is essential to ensure implementation.

It is a good idea to involve middle and senior management in a separate programme to take them through what is being planned for the frontline ranks. In fact, unless the senior management of the organization comes out very strongly in favour of bringing about the change, it is unlikely that the change will ever come about. This is true of any cultural shift. It must begin at the top. Take a simple thing like punctuality. If senior management is not punctual, it will be very difficult to ensure that the rank and file consider punctuality important. Leading by example is the most powerful way of affecting change.

The strongest WIIFM for change comes from immediate supervisors and the leadership of the company. When employees believe that smiling at a customer and greeting them is noticed by their boss, the change takes place very quickly. Why should the need for a greeting be treated any differently from a sales target? After all, it is the smile that will bring the customer back!

Senior managers can be given some input on assessment skills, coaching and giving feedback. They can then form a supervision army within the organization that will be able to spot any inconsistencies in the sound of service at a micro level. It also puts the pressure on them to act it out as well. Commitment to the initiative will form the difference between success and failure.

External Quality Control

A useful strategy to complement the change initiative can be using the services of a third party quality auditor. By using techniques such as mystery shopping, customer surveys, employee surveys and focus group discussions, a quality check can be conducted on measuring the degree of adherence to the parameters laid down in the sound of service.

Data from external quality monitoring services is valuable because it is unbiased and objective. It allows companies to get early-warning signals of lacunae in their service delivery and take corrective action before real damage takes place. Being involved in the early stages of the choice of strategy for quality monitoring and the actual questionnaires that will be used in the surveys ensures that there is a meeting of goals of the service provider and the client, and extremely useful insights can be obtained.

The sound of service is an idea who's time has come. Companies need to distinguish themselves in a crowded marketplace and the only way they can do this is through the relationship they build with their customers. Each interaction the customer has with the company is a moment of truth—whether it will be a moment of magic or a moment of misery, is the choice the company needs to make.

The Last Word

In the final analysis, it is CRM which is the differentiator in an increasingly commoditized world.

The challenge is to define the customer-shareholder, internal, trade, or consumer and then devise strategies and places to delight them and implement these plans.

Devise systems that facilitate the various customer groups to speak with you—open the channels of communications/develop an environment where the concept of internal customer service flourishes, and those in the frontline dealing with trade and consumers are empowered to delight them. With a multitude of brands and new ones appearing everyday, market share is not enough.

We need our customers to be not just users but brand advocates. We must give them reason to be advocates. Emotional satisfaction besides product delivery. In a word, only by delighting customers can we hope to retain his/her custom.

Appendix

Technology—Paving the Road to CRM

THE CRM methodology requires creation of an enterprise-wide database, containing all information about your customer. This enables all individuals who have contact with the customer to know everything that is taking place with the customer.

What Does CRM Require?

As mentioned above, CRM requires a central enterprise-wide database that is used by all members of the organization. The first relationship generally occurs during the sales and marketing cycle, when the 'customer' is first a 'prospect'. During the sales process, all information gathered about the prospect and their personnel is recorded in the CRM database. Once the prospect becomes a customer, sales will most likely still retain a relationship with the customer. In addition, customer support, professional services, development, and management play important roles in providing service and maintaining a good relationship with the customer.

What CRM Software Does

Every conversation, visit, or correspondence with a customer should be recorded in this database. You need to track the individuals as your customer, the products which the customer has purchased, what has been shipped to the customer, maintenance contracts or service-level agreements, as well as all work or support provided to your customer.

If all relationships and contacts are maintained in this database, any person who is speaking with the customer will have access to all this information. Not only does this improve the ability to provide superior service, but each customer feels as if they are important to you, which results in higher customer satisfaction.

What are the Components and Who are the Users of a CRM System?

- ◆ Marketing needs to analyse previous marketing campaigns to determine where marketing rupees should be spent. They should be able to identify the type, size, etc., of their ideal prospect.

- Sales Force Automation (SFA) is crucial for tele-sales and/or outside sales force to automate their sales effort. This should include tracking a history of each sales opportunity and the ability to set ticklers, do forecasting, track the competition and all other available information about the prospect.
- Once the prospect becomes a customer, you need to record the products purchased, quantities, maintenance contracts, and/or service-level agreements. You will also need to track the products that have been shipped to the customer. This might include the version/release for software products and the serial numbers for hardware products.
- Customer support comes into the picture to provide service for the customer in answering questions, resolving bugs, and tracking enhancement requests. During this process, the support representative should be notified if the customer's maintenance contract has expired. They also need to be aware of all other open issues for this customer.
- Development and quality assurance are involved when the customer's issue is an actual software bug. Development needs to record the way they are fixing this problem and how the fix is being supplied to the customer.
- Professional services maintains a relationship with the customer to provide implementation services, training, custom modifications, or other consulting services. All this information should be recorded in the CRM database to provide a

complete picture of all contacts and services provided to the customer.

◆ Management must be able to review and monitor the services and interactions with customers. An automated escalation or notification system should warn management if response times, or other time commitments are not being met.

Some CRM technologies (based on research on websites) are mentioned below, as they 'sell themselves'.

Innovative eMarketing Solutions

InterlinkONE's web-based eMarketing software is the most innovative suite of integrated marketing solutions available. The suite combines traditional marketing initiatives and electronic programmes resulting in an effective marketing mix, producing the most productive outcome possible. The eMarketing Suite includes functions and features, which support all aspects of successful marketing programmes.

Some features include:

◆ campaign management;
◆ lead management;
◆ list and contact management;
◆ email blast management;
◆ electronic distribution of marketing materials;
◆ marketing project management;
◆ order fulfillment management.

Campaign Management

Optimize the allocation of marketing rupees by focusing on segments and marketing vehicles proven to produce a return. Manage multi-tiered campaigns using easy to understand visual tools. Capture responses electronically by building online response forms with no programming experience required.

Campaign Management Highlights

- complex campaigns made easy;
- multi-tiered management for improved decision making;
- immediate campaign execution and measurement;
- direct campaigns based on target markets and segments;
- effectively manage marketing rupees.

Web-based response forms developed in minutes automate the acquisition of new leads by monitoring campaigns in a simple to understand graphical structure. Drive multi-tiered campaigns that are designed to fit your unique marketing mix, including all channels and vehicle for communicating your message. Target the most profitable segments by focusing on the most successful marketing vehicles.

Lead Management

Manage how leads are distributed to your sales force. Administer lead-weighting criteria based on your rules, allowing your team to focus their energies on opportunities, which are most likely to generate revenue. Track leads through the entire marketing process and decide when leads are routed to sales, based on event triggered point assignments.

Lead Management Highlights

- modify response from questions and answers in real time;
- set weighting for lead qualification;
- associate marketing collateral for immediate distribution;
- manage lead distribution using simple interface.

Intelligent distribution based on your business rules generate online response forms quickly and easily, using a simple web-based tool attaching results to your campaigns. Qualify lead inquiries immediately, based on scoring criteria that you define. Automate the distribution of inquiries by applying rules unique to your business.

List and Contact Management

Built-in capabilities to manage contacts and segments. Automate marketing and sales initiatives, develop targeted lists, prioritize contacts and lists, capture communications, develop forecasts and pipeline reporting, improve time management, organize schedules.

List and Contact Management Highlights

- generate lists for targeted initiatives;
- manage opt-in/opt-out lists and inactive contacts;

- administer fields to align with campaigns;
- complex lists pulled instantly.

Facilitate email blast distribution in seconds. Manage targeted list of your contacts and manage future activities. Query for lists, based on simple or complex requirements. Save lists and manage the marketing cycle for individual segments.

Email Blast Management

Develop HTML and text emails. Insert pictures, logos and colours for professional looking emails that grab readers' attention. Pre-designed templates ensure no design or HTML knowledge is required. Manage pre-scheduled email blasts such as monthly newsletters, press releases, client updates, or seminar invitations.

Email Blast Management Highlights

- personalize messages and define email content;
- embed campaign response forms;
- embed documentation in message body preventing bounce backs;
- send as HTML or text to accommodate all email systems.

Intelligent distribution automatically eliminates opt- Send targeted email blasts that account for and track opt-in/ opt-out lists. Reach more prospects and improve campaigns response rates by personalizing and tailoring the content of your email. Develop dynamic, media-rich email messages with the flexibility to populate pre-defined templates or upload custom HTML.

Marketing Project Management

Improve the efficiency of marketing projects and increase team productivity. Create campaign project plans, manage campaign schedules and tasks, control related documentation, generate Gantt charts, monitor milestones and deadlines, and use event-triggered email alerts.

Marketing Project Management Highlights

- facilitate project collaboration over the web;
- track project deliverables, milestones and schedules;
- improve accountability and productivity;
- view task history in centralized location.

Maintain document version controls. Create detailed marketing projects outlining tasks, deliverables and milestones. Communicate with team members in a virtual environment to ensure priorities are managed and tasks are completed. Manage documentation and allow team members to edit and manage content.

 Applied Innovation Management

 HelpDesk Expert for Customer Service

Features/Highlights

✔ *100 Per Cent Web-based*

With AIM's 100 per cent web-based HelpDesk Expert for customer service solutions, there's absolutely no client-side software or plug-ins to install—ever. HelpDesk Expert for Customer Service is installed on a web server, so customers and support staff can access the system from anywhere, anytime with any standard web browser.

✔ *Flexible Workflow*

The system uses a flexible scheme to accommodate any organizations' workflow, and can be set up for both automatic and manual ticket routing.

✔ Extensive Charts and Reports

Charts and reports can be generated to easily measure trends in support, including metrics on the number, type and frequency of problems reported and solved. Managers can print any ticket to have a hard copy of an issue for easy reference.

✔ Rule-based Email and Paging Notification

The system makes sure no trouble tickets go unnoticed—staff members can be automatically paged or emailed to ensure all tickets are taken care of immediately based on certain rules.

✔ Whiteboard

Staff can post information about new releases, service packs, security alerts and updates, so that customers are presented with the information when they log into the support centre.

✔ Chat System (Chat4Help)

Integrates with web chat system that enhances customer satisfaction and increases online sales conversions.

✔ Supports File Attachments

AIM's HelpDesk Expert for customer service allows users or staff to attach an unlimited number of any type of files to a ticket, easily expanding the amount of information associated with an incident. A picture is worth a thousand words, with screenshots of problems or logs of error messages, support staff can have all problem information accessible to them with a simple click of the mouse.

✔ Dynamic Frequently Asked Questions (FAQs)

Create custom FAQs based on tickets submitted to your custom database.

✔ Download Centre

Staff can upload files into the download centre library so that customers can easily download needed items. Post manuals, brochures—virtually any file accessible to both your customers and staff.

✔ Microsoft Excel Spread Sheet Integration

HelpDesk Expert for Customer Service is tightly integrated with Microsoft Excel. The system can generate Excel spread sheets to include all reports and charts.

Epicor offers award-winning CRM solutions that enable you to have full visibility of your customer relationship so that you can provide improved levels of service to your most important asset.

- make sure you are spending your marketing rupees on programmes that generate results;
- focus your sales teams on the right opportunities;
- increase the effectiveness of your sales team to close business faster;
- gain visibility to your sales forecast;
- more efficiently manage support calls;
- increase responsiveness by providing effective customer self-service solutions via the Internet.

Epicor's CRM solutions provide you with the flexibility and functionality you need to better manage your customer relationships.

Clientele delivers highly regarded CRM solutions used by thousands of companies. Clientele allows businesses to better communicate, track and build relationships with customers. Offering both CRM and internal helpdesk solutions, with more than 10 years experience and over 3,000 customers, Epicor supplies small and midsize enterprises with everything they need for a successful implementation: quality products, experienced professional services, and excellent support.

On Contact CRM Solution

We all know it's much more profitable for a company to retain and keep existing customers than it is to go out and find new customers. So, shouldn't you do everything you can to build a strong customer service relationship with *your* customers?

- call escalation, smart-query keyword searches and automated incident and problem reporting are some of the exclusive features CMS provides;
- geared to help your customer service professionals interact with your customers.

As a salesperson you want a tool that gives you quick and easy access to all the information you need about your accounts. With CMS, you have total control to efficiently manage all your prospects and customers.

- easy to use central starting point provides quick access to complete account picture;
- one click takes you to where you need to go;
- a quick and easy view of every interaction is displayed;
- store unlimited amount of information (e.g., contacts, phone number, notes, etc.);
- customize look and feel with CMS Form Painter.

Talisma CRM Solutions

The Talisma® eCRM Suite is developed from a single code base, enabling a level of integration and interoperability unmatched in the industry. Talisma interaction-centric CRM solutions integrate all communication channels across multiple touch points, including phone, email, web self-help, web forms, chat, VoIP, fax, wireless, and face-to-face meetings. The company also provides extensive integration, education, and outsourced staffing services. Talisma Support Services compliments its full suite of CRM offerings providing skilled and knowledge-able people to meet any company's need for 24×7 world-wide support. Talisma's proven philosophy of rapid soft-ware deployment and use-based evolution has helped hundreds of companies create long-lasting and profitable customer relationships and see early returns on their in-vestment. Whether hosted or installed, modular Talisma® eCRM products and services are easy to deploy, extend, integrate, and scale.

Security and Administration

All pages within your CRM software solution are located on SSL to encrypt and protect your precious data. All of our database servers are backed up on a regular, tight schedule every day. We will take care of the backing up of your data on a daily basis, removing another chore from your daily routine.

Users of the CRM software solution possess various levels of access, examples include:

- super users—access to all data;
- managers—access to all data for a group;
- users—access to their own data;
- special users—access to selected data in read only.

All of these access levels are configurable by you (by the super user) from within your CRM software package. In addition, super users can also configure other lists with the CRM software, including organization and user cat-egories, industry sectors, services provided, and transac-tion types.

Structure of the Data

The core structure of the CRM software solution is:

- ◆ Organization data—Organization details can be stored within defined categories.
- ◆ Contacts—Contacts are the core records and contain as much detail as you require.
- ◆ Transactions—Records anything that happens with a contact.

Transactions are the core of the CRM software solution. The manager of the system (super user) can define the types of transactions available to users. Recording transactions can be simple or very sophisticated.

A sophisticated transaction can be anything from a training record to a billing request. Sophisticated transactions are constructed by strategies according to your specific requirements.

Talisma Contact Center Suite

The Talisma Contact Center Suite features:

- ◆ A unified agent desktop, which allows CSRs to communicate with customers through all communication channels, including phone, email, web chat, VoIP, and so on, in an integrated fashion keeping a single, comprehensive view of each customer.
- ◆ Powerful reporting and analytic capabilities that uncover valuable business intelligence and enable you to take immediate action. Intuitive reports provide key metrics on customer behaviour and operations, and allow you to easily evaluate

response time, workforce efficiency, and other critical performance factors.

♦ Decision makers throughout your organization have instant access to the information they need to improve customer identification, acquisition, retention, and growth—vital elements of increased economic performance.

♦ The software you select will naturally depend upon your particular needs and the commercial terms on offer. However, software alone is not enough. It is its usage and acceptance that is key and this usage and acceptance must be enterprise-wide.

♦ Therefore, it is important that top management not only believe in CRM but practice it, and see that it is being implemented systematically.

Siebel

Siebel Systems is one of the leading providers of CRM software and a leading provider of software applications for business intelligence and business integration. Through its 'CRM for Everyone' strategy, Siebel provides CRM software for any kind of organization, any type of user.

Siebel Systems has proven its ability to address the major issues facing IT organizations and consultants today: reducing the cost and time of implementation and integration, aligning your organization around the business change, and achieving your business objectives with a faster return-on-investment (ROI) and a lower total cost of ownership.

CRM Customer Success Staples Business Delivery, Teleservices has improved its ability to develop and execute outbound campaigns, increased its margins, and increased overall outbound talk times by 22 per cent.

Application Platform Highlights

- Increase productivity and accelerate end-user adoption due to simplicity and user-friendly platform.
- Application can be operated via the keyboard for the convenience of the user.
- Microsoft outlook and exchange integration as synchronization of data between outlook. Siebel does not require any action from end users.
- Has the ability to display completed activities on the calendar as well as scheduled activities.
- Link a contact or opportunity to a meeting or activity.
- Application can utilize Microsoft Word, Excel and Power Point.
- Marketing campaign management.
- Ability to measure campaign effectiveness, campaign cost, campaign letters, envelopes, labels, can manage email campaigns and fax-blast campaigns, can create scripts and manage telemarketing campaigns.
- Can automatically allocate calls to telemarketers by rules such as 'round robin' and queuing.
- Telemarketing call scripts can be developed and maintained within the application.
- Software will automatically rate leads according to user defined criteria for qualification and/or risk analysis.

- Ability to generate forms such as mailing labels and envelopes.
- Forecasting aggregation ability for management to rollup sales forecast data into summary level data according to user-definable criteria such as team, region, etc.
- Manager can override the forecast at the opportunity level (dollars and probabilities) without changing the original.
- Sales quotas can be assigned by territory, region, division, and/or as territories are defined.
- Auto-assignment: The software automatically assigns and notifies a rep of a new lead tracking.
- Built in ability to track lead source sales productivity.
- Integration to one or more ERP (back office accounting) applications is supported by the CRM software developer.
- Ability to 'promote' prospect to customer so that back office accounting system is automatically populated with customer information.
- Ability to view accounts receivable aging from accounting system in real time or near real time without customization.
- Ability to view customer's document history, credit notes, payments, aging, etc., from within CRM system.
- Can check inventory availability; integrates with accounting system.
- Can support multiple inventory locations per quote or sales order.
- Can generate a credit invoice, including the refund entry for accounts payable.

- Maintains multiple versions of proposal or multiple proposals for an opportunity.
- Provides graphical analysis of data for marketing, sales, and customer service info.
- Application can 'guide' the user according to customer-specific business processes that can vary based on type of opportunity, etc., and can be specified in the application.
- Ability to manage access to software screens, features, etc., via groups.
- Security can be controlled at the field level.
- Can create and manage email within application.
- Can create and manage individual and group calendars, or integrates to Outlook.
- CTI (Computer Telephony Integration) Software will automatically pop-up the contact record when call is received or transferred.
- Wireless supports wireless PDA access.
- Supports SMS.
- Uses the most widely accepted general reporting tool.
- Supports easy integration of inquiries via the web without user intervention.
- Can export and import data to Microsoft Office applications.
- Documented commitment to data integrity and backup.

Index